FAITH AND THE CREEDS

Christian Belief for Everyone

Book 1

FAITH AND THE CREEDS

Alister McGrath

First published in Great Britain in 2013

Society for Promoting Christian Knowledge
36 Causton Street
London SW1P 4ST
www.spckpublishing.co.uk

British Library Cataloguing-in-Publication Data
A catalogue record for this book is available from the British Library

ISBN 978–0–281–06833–3
eBook ISBN 978–0–281–06834–0

Typeset by Graphicraft Limited, Hong Kong
First printed in Great Britain by Ashford Colour Press
Subsequently digitally printed in Great Britain

eBook by Graphicraft Limited

Produced on paper from sustainable forests

Contents

Introduction

What do Christians believe? Why do they believe this? And what difference does it make? In the *Christian Belief for Everyone* series, I aim to explore the basic themes of a simple and genuinely Christian faith.

I have been persuaded of the need for this new series through personal conversations with many, both inside and outside Christianity. Ordinary churchgoers have often told me that they wrestle with their faith, being perfectly prepared to trust God, but not so sure about some of the Church's ways of talking about him. Other Christians have spoken of how they are frequently puzzled by some of their beliefs, like the doctrine of the Trinity, while many outside the faith have indicated that they are intrigued by the new way of seeing things that such doctrines make possible. My discussions with those who do not believe have often taken unexpected turns: I remember my delight after one particular conversation with an atheist in Australia, in which I explained what the Trinity was all about. 'That makes sense!' he declared. 'Tell me more.'

The 'big picture' of the Christian faith that I aim to set out in this series is something that makes sense both of what we see around us and what we experience within. Traditional introductions to Christian belief have tended to treat its ideas – such as incarnation or redemption or the creeds (to which we will return later) – as if each is a little box or watertight compartment, unconnected to any other, to be opened up and explored individually. I would like to take a different approach, one that emphasizes the importance of seeing the whole, not just examining its constituent elements, because it seems to me that in order to appreciate individual beliefs, you need to see the big picture of which they are part. So in this first volume we will begin with the 'panorama', as it were; then in the next four volumes we will move on to the 'snapshots', as we look at individual beliefs in more detail. Of course, I will not manage to cover everything, but I hope those interested in Christianity's core themes will find that they really want to go on to explore them more thoroughly.

As I am writing primarily for 'ordinary' Christians rather than professional theologians or clergy, it seems fitting to draw on three of the great lay theologians of the twentieth century – G. K. Chesterton (1874–1936), C. S. Lewis (1898–1963) and Dorothy L. Sayers (1893–1957). These writers each showed a remarkable ability to grasp the essence of Christianity, to express it in ways that connect up with everyday life – through powerful prose, memorable stories and vivid analogies – and to defend it to those who doubted.

Chesterton was a journalist, noted for his Father Brown novels, who captured the imagination of his readers with his winsome accounts of the Christian faith. Sayers, one of the most renowned writers of crime fiction of her age, found that her faith helped her make sense of the biggest mystery of all – the meaning of life. And Lewis, a former atheist who discovered Christianity through reading great literature, went on to express his faith in works that, in turn, became classics. All three will be our travelling companions as we explore the landscape of faith, and try to grasp the new way of seeing that it makes possible.

In fact, the approach of this series is similar to that adopted by Lewis in his *Mere Christianity* (1952). Lewis drew a helpful distinction between the common, shared assumptions of the Christian faith, and their more specific interpretation by individual denominations. He asked his readers to imagine a large hall, with doors leading to various rooms. The hall, for Lewis, represented the simple, consensual faith that underlies Christianity – what he himself termed 'mere Christianity'. The rooms represented particular ways of understanding and applying this basic Christianity – the various denominations that have developed over the centuries, each with its own distinctive approach to living out the faith. Like Lewis, I will be exploring a consensual, basic Christianity, using accessible and engaging language and images. I will leave it to you to work out for yourself where this may take you in terms of your denominational commitments.

Later books in this series will look at aspects of Christian thinking, such as its understanding of the nature of God, and of the identity and significance of Jesus of Nazareth. But for now, let's concentrate on the place and purpose of personal faith and public creeds. What do Christians mean when they say they 'believe in God'? Why do we use creeds? Can't we just trust in God and get on with life? These are all fair questions, and I hope we can come up with some helpful answers.

This series of books is dedicated to the people of the Shill Valley and Broadshire benefice in west Oxfordshire, consisting of the churches in the Cotswold villages of Alvescot, Black Bourton, Broadwell, Broughton Poggs, Filkins, Holwell,

Kelmscott, Kencot, Langford, Little Faringdon, Shilton and Westwell. It has been my privilege to minister to those village congregations for the past five years, and much of the material in this series has been adapted from sermons preached during that period.

Alister McGrath

1

The journey: clues to the meaning of the universe

I was cycling round France with some student friends. One particularly hot day, we decided to rest for a while by the side of a country road. As I filled my water bottle from a nearby pump, I noticed a man walking briskly along, his arms swinging from side to side with military precision.

Noticing the pump, he stopped, and waited for me to finish. I politely asked him where he was heading. 'Nowhere!' he told me. Regular walks, he declared, were his way of distracting himself from the meaninglessness of life. 'I'm not going anywhere. I'm just passing time.' A few moments later, I watched him striding defiantly into the distance, head held high, on his journey to nowhere in particular.

Life is a journey. That's just the way things are, whether you believe in God or not. We are travelling along a mysterious road, wondering how to make sense of it. Does it lead anywhere important? Come to think of it, does it lead *anywhere*? And what are we meant to be doing as we journey?

Writers have been pondering such questions since the dawn of civilization. When all's said and done, I would like to suggest that there are really only two possible responses.

For the first, let's turn to the French atheist philosopher Jean-Paul Sartre (1905–80). He shaped the thinking of many bright young things in the 1960s and had no doubt about the meaning of life: there was none. Everything that exists 'is born without reason, prolongs itself out of weakness, and dies by chance'.[1] Existence is pointless and meaningless. 'Here we sit, all of us, eating and drinking to preserve our precious existence and really there is nothing, nothing, absolutely no reason for existing.'[2]

It is a view with which the stranger I met in France would have had much sympathy. It is also shared by the world's best-known atheist, Richard Dawkins (born 1941), author of *The God Delusion* and one of the founders of the 'New Atheism'. At the heart of the universe, he declares, there is 'no design, no purpose, no evil and no good, nothing but blind pitiless indifference'.[3] We have no reason to live, other than to propagate our genes. We're walking along a road that goes nowhere.

Inflexible atheism of this kind takes it for granted that there is no God, no transcendent realm, and no 'big story' to make sense of things. What explanation, then, can it offer for why so many people believe in God? Dawkins's answer is as simple as it is dogmatic: people of faith are *deluded*. They are small-minded individuals, unable to cope with the harsh reality of a bleak and pointless universe, who therefore resort to inventing meaning to console themselves.

I used to think that way myself. I assumed that intelligent people knew that there was no God, no meaning, no purpose to life, and that only fools believed otherwise. It made me feel good to be part of this intellectual and cultural elite. I know it sounds very smug and arrogant, but I took great pleasure in looking down on those around me who believed in God, and priding myself on being more intelligent and sophisticated than they were.

At school, one of my most vivid memories was looking out of the dormitory windows at night. When it wasn't raining, I could see the stars, like pinpoints of light on a black velvet cloth. But although I was often overwhelmed by the sheer beauty of the night sky, darker thoughts distracted me. The immensity of the universe seemed to stress my own insignificance. What was I, set in this great context? The answer was obvious: nothing.

Yet there is a second way of looking at things. What if the universe is actually studded with clues as to its meaning? What if those clues lead to a gateway for discovering a deeper order of things and our place within it? This view, which I eventually came to hold, stresses that the true meaning of reality is to know God, and that once we have grasped this, we can begin to make sense of our lives. There really is a 'big picture' and we are an important part of it. In fact, the world is so richly signposted with hints and rumours of the divine that atheists simply have to turn down the lights to give their unbelief a chance!

We will return to this central theme of a big picture of reality shortly. For now, we need to explore just where the idea of 'faith' fits in.

What is faith?

For some more excitable atheists, the word 'faith' is like a red rag to a bull. All faith is blind faith! As the journalist Christopher Hitchens (1949–2011), who became a leading defender of atheism in his later years, boldly declared, 'our belief is not a belief'.[4] In other words, Hitchens would only accept what could be *proved* to be right. In his view, religious people run away from reality, refusing to offer any kind of intellectual justification for what they believe, while science and logic both prove their ideas.

It's a neat and simple creed. But is it right? More interestingly, can it be maintained? As his numerous critics pointed out, Hitchens's writings were full of assertions that couldn't be proved, especially when it came to questions of morality and religious belief. I've no doubt that he thought he was right. But many of his bold statements lack any evidential foundation, and this is also true of the work of Richard Dawkins. As the cultural critic Terry Eagleton (born 1943) so devastatingly observed in a scathing review, 'Dawkins lives more by faith than by reason.'

No one, however, would disagree with Hitchens when he asserts that mathematics and logic are subjects in which it is possible to prove that something is right. The following statements are completely reliable and trustworthy:

$2 + 2 = 4$
The whole is greater than the part.

Sadly, it's virtually impossible to prove things to be true in any other area of life. We can certainly give good reasons for believing, for example, that rape is wrong, or that democracy is better than fascism, but these things just can't be verified.

Anyway, how significant are these truths of logic and mathematics? Why would someone poised on the brink of taking his own life put the revolver away on being told that the whole is greater than the part? Or pour the cyanide down the sink when she was informed that $2 + 2 = 4$? These statements may be factually correct. They are, however, existentially insignificant, having nothing to say about the deepest questions of the human mind or the yearnings of the human heart.

I can verify that $2 + 2 = 4$. But I can't prove that life is meaningful. Nor can I substantiate the core theme of the United Nations 1948 Universal Declaration of Human Rights: 'All human beings are born free and equal in dignity and rights.' Nor can I prove that there is a God. I can certainly give some good reasons for *believing* that these convictions are correct – but neither I nor anyone else can demonstrate that they *are*. Only shallow truths can be proved. The deepest truths of life lie beyond ultimate confirmation. The simple fact is that none of us, whether religious or secular, can prove *any* of the great truths we live by. That's just the way life is.

What about science? Here, I have to confess a personal interest. I developed a love for the natural sciences when I was young, and even built a little telescope so that I could see deep into space. Awe-struck, I longed to know more about the mysteries of the universe. I went on to specialize in the sciences at high school, before going up to Oxford University to take a first degree in chemistry and then do research in molecular biology. For a while, I believed that science (which I will always love) might help me work out what life was all about.

But I discovered that it *didn't*. And then I realized that it *couldn't*. Science helps us uncover the hidden logic of our cosmic system, but that's not the same as telling us why it exists and where we fit in. Although Richard Dawkins and I disagree on many points, I am completely at one with him when he states that 'science has no methods for deciding what is ethical'.[5] Meaning and value are not things that can be 'read off' the world. Science is good at taking things to pieces. But analysis is not enough. What really matters is what we do with these pieces. We need synthesis in order to perceive the big picture. Science dismantles so that we can see how things work; faith reassembles so that we can see what they mean.

The great German sociologist Max Weber (1864–1920) argued that early twentieth-century western culture was becoming obsessed with what he termed 'rationalization'. Everything, influential voices declared, had to be proved, and science was the best way of proving things. Weber had difficulty in taking this seriously. Surely only a child would think that the natural sciences could answer life's great questions about meaning or purpose? Weber made rather caustic remarks about adults who seemed to be locked into juvenile ways of thinking about science that could no longer be sustained:

> Who – apart from certain big children who are indeed found in the natural sciences – still believes that the findings of astronomy, biology, physics or chemistry could teach us anything about the *meaning* of the world?[6]

Weber had a still deeper concern here. An exaggerated emphasis on human reason was actually trapping people within an 'iron cage' of rationality. They were allowing themselves to be imprisoned by reason, in the sense that they could only accept things that could be *proved*. And that, Weber suggested, was leading to a very limited and inadequate grasp of reality. Humanity needed to be liberated from the rationalist prison it had created for itself.

There are still people today who talk about being 'guided' by reason when they are actually being constricted by it.

They are desperate to limit reality to the very small and dull world of what reason can prove.

When I was an atheist, I tried to console myself by imagining that my atheism was an act of bravery and defiance. Atheism was so unappealing and unattractive that nobody would believe it – unless, of course, it was right. I know it sounds weird, but the drabness of a godless world became a reason for trusting that I was on the right track.

In fact, I was really just skimming the surface of life, accepting an arbitrary limit on my knowledge and refusing to go deeper. Believing that 'what you see is what you get' can be an excuse to be intellectually lazy and unadventurous. It's like looking out to sea over a coral lagoon, and registering nothing but an expanse of turquoise water. Yet beneath the surface others are scuba-diving, taking delight in the coral reefs and the exotic and brightly coloured fish darting from ridge to ridge. None of this is visible from the surface, but it exists, waiting to be discovered.

It is not surprising that old-fashioned rationalism, which limits reality to what can be proved by logic and mathematics, has been given such a hard time in recent years. Most people are now willing to draw a much-needed distinction between 'thin' and 'thick' approaches to reason. The 'thin' approach limits knowledge to the proven abstract ideas of logic and mathematics, while the 'thick' approach recognizes the numerous beliefs that human beings may reasonably own, without being able to prove them by the highly restrictive methods of logic. 'We hold many beliefs that have no unimpeachably rational justification, but are nonetheless reasonable to entertain' (Terry Eagleton).

Imagine seeing a photograph of a beautiful valley and just knowing that's where you want to live. This is the world that reason, when rightly understood, is able to open up to us. Applied to faith, reason helps us recognize the big picture that makes sense of the world and our lives. This means that we don't need to launch ourselves on a random flight of imagination to believe certain things are true, or fling ourselves into the arms of a non-existent God we've conjured up as a way of coping with life! Rather, we can come to faith through carefully worked out arguments, or by leaps of the imagination based on our deepest intuitions. Some of us will be drawn to God by the quest for personal stability and significance, others by the sheer beauty of the things of God. All these approaches are valid. Think of them as individual threads woven together in a tapestry of faith.

C. S. Lewis discovered something of this richness when he moved away from what he termed his early 'glib and shallow rationalism' as an atheist. Pure reason offered him a bleak intellectual landscape that he could not bear to inhabit. Yet this, his intellect insisted, was all that there was. To believe otherwise was pure fantasy. Yet Lewis's imagination taught him that there had to be more. 'Nearly all that I loved I believed to be imaginary; nearly all that I believed to be real I thought grim and meaningless.'[7] And in the end, Lewis discovered a way of thinking that allowed him to weave together reason and imagination, and opened the way to his reconnection with God.

It's a fascinating story,[8] and we need to tell it in a little more detail.

Finding the big picture

Lewis became an atheist in his teenage years, bombarding his Christian friends with the 'thin artillery of a seventeen year old rationalist'.[9] His aggressive atheism was deepened by his experiences during the First World War, when he was wounded while leading an infantry attack in April 1918. His poetry of that period rages against a silent God, who cared nothing for the suffering of the world. After the war, Lewis went to Oxford to begin his academic career, initially studying the thought and literature of the ancient world, and then English literature.

Gradually, he came to see that his earlier way of thinking, which he had believed simple, was merely simplistic. Reading the classics of western literature reopened questions he assumed to be closed. 'A young man who wishes to remain a sound Atheist cannot be too careful of his reading. There are traps everywhere',[10] he wrote in his autobiography, *Surprised by Joy*. Lewis had no desire to believe in God. Yet he eventually found himself compelled to do so. And having become a 'most reluctant convert', he went on to explore and explain what it was about Christianity that he found so compelling and transforming.

Many would agree that Lewis offers an intelligent, reflective and winsome account of the Christian faith. Yet why might his account be so attractive? His Oxford colleague Austin Farrer (1904–68), a distinguished philosopher of religion, put his finger on the answer. Lewis, he remarked, makes us 'think we are listening to an argument', when in reality 'we are presented with a vision, and it is the vision that carries conviction'.[11]

I know what Farrer meant. A few years ago, I was in Amsterdam attending a conference, when I found myself with enough time between lectures to visit an art gallery. I ended up going to the Van Gogh Museum and wandered happily through the exhibit halls. Every now and then, I paused by paintings that seemed to stand out – like Van Gogh's 1890 work *Wheatfield with Crows*. I was drawn to this painting, and began to look at it from multiple angles. I admired Van Gogh's brushstrokes and the rich and brilliant palette of colours that he used. But what drew me to the painting was its totality – its combination of patterns, colours and textures. Because I liked it, I wanted to know more about it. Having only limited time, I had walked past other paintings that did not have the same effect on me. Something about this one made me stop and examine it in more detail.

Lewis was drawn to Christianity not so much by the individual arguments in its favour as by its compelling 'big picture' vision of reality. It seemed to make sense of everything that really mattered to him and it connected with his inner longing for truth, beauty and goodness. As Lewis recalled, his atheism drove him to the conclusion that everything he loved and valued had to be rejected as 'imaginary'. The few things this dogmatic atheism allowed him to believe turned out to be 'grim and meaningless'. It was heartbreaking. But the Christian way of looking at things made sense of his hopes and longings – the things in life that he really cared about. It affirmed that they were *real*, and that they were *important*. As the pieces began to fall into place, Lewis realized that this landscape of faith he was exploring was the world he was meant to inhabit.

Lewis's approach is one that many natural scientists would accept, resonating strongly, as it does, with their own working methods. A theory is to be judged against observations, by how well it can account for what we see and experience around and within us. Of course, there may be some loose ends. In places things may be a little fuzzy. Yet what really matters is that a good theory helps us make more sense of a complex and confusing world. As human beings, we are always going to be drawn to ways of thinking that illuminate and inspire.

Consider legal dramas and crime fiction. Every great crime writer teases their readers about the solution to the mystery they have created. None of the clues they offer is enough on its own, but considered together, they have a cumulative force that points towards a conclusion. It may not be possible to prove the conclusion absolutely, but there's little doubt about what the best explanation of the clues might be. So we might recognize the fingerprints of God in the ordering of the natural world and in the deepest intuitions of human nature, and conclude that these clues call out to be woven together to allow us to see a bigger picture.

The philosopher Michael Polanyi (1891–1976) offered one of the most penetrating accounts of the philosophical implications and consequences of the scientific method (which may be defined as 'a logical and rational order of steps by which scientists come to conclusions about the world around them'). For Polanyi, it was clear that the 'pursuit of discovery' was 'guided by sensing the presence of a hidden reality toward which our clues are pointing'.[12] Polanyi's insight is easily illustrated from the history of science. For example, Isaac Newton (1643–1727) came to realize that there was a common 'hidden reality' lying behind the motions of bodies on earth – such as the falling of an apple from a tree – and the movement of the planets round the sun.

Newton called this invisible, intangible, hidden reality 'gravity'. He was never quite sure that he really believed in the notion, but it seemed to make a lot more sense of his observations than anything else he could come up with. In the end, he was convinced it was right. Its ability to explain was an indication of its truth. In a famous image, he pointed to a greater reality lying beyond and behind what could be perceived:

> I seem to have been only like a small boy playing on the sea-shore, diverting myself in now and then finding a smoother pebble or a prettier shell than the ordinary, whilst the great ocean of truth lay all undiscovered before me.[13]

Many, like Newton, have longed to see into that ocean of truth and map its depths. Or to return to the analogy we're exploring, to find a trustworthy big picture that weaves together the threads of our experience and shows how we fit into the universe, culture and history.

We often feel overwhelmed by the complex world around us. There's so much to take in. Is it just a jumble of facts? A collection of random pieces of information? Or is there something that holds it all together, that connects everything up? The Swiss theologian Emil Brunner (1889–1966) once wrote about looking down on the city of Zurich from a nearby mountain. It was night, and the shimmering sea of light he saw below him was vast and apparently random in design. But, he remarked, the city's professional electricians would be able to make perfect sense of the pattern of lights. They would have the diagrams that explained what was going on.

The Christian faith allows us to see patterns in this apparent chaos of our world; to perceive a melody when others only hear a noise. Instead of being overwhelmed with *information*, we are enabled to discern *meaning*. The American poet Edna St Vincent Millay (1892–1950) expressed the universal quest for meaning in terms of making sense of 'a meteoric shower of facts' raining from the sky. These 'facts' are like pieces of a jigsaw that need to be assembled, allowing us to discover the Christian big picture, which gives us a framework for understanding things and a basis for working out what we ought to be doing. Everyone has a big picture, whether they realize it or not. It's just that some people have a very *small* big picture, as we saw earlier, which limits reality to the cold realm of logic.

A quick return to crime fiction might be helpful here. Imagine that you're reading a detective novel – perhaps one of Agatha Christie's cliff-hangers. We come to the final scene – the great denouement, in which Hercule Poirot or Miss Marple gathers all the potential suspects together. Then the great detective sketches the big picture that explains the clues and links them together. Hercule Poirot tells the story of what really happened leading up to the murder on the Orient Express, and Miss Marple what led up to the appearance of a mysterious body in the library. This big picture does more than identify the murderer: it makes sense of all the clues. They are like threads, woven into its fabric. Things that once made no sense at all now do because they are seen in the right way.

To emphasize the importance of grasping this big picture, we shall now consider two of the deepest human intuitions – the heart's desire, and our sense of moral obligation – and reflect on how these fit into the Christian way of seeing things.

The heart's desire

A friend of mine left England some years ago to take up work in the United States. He liked living there but never really settled. Deep within, a little echo of a voice kept murmuring,

'This isn't where you belong. This isn't where you're meant to be.' The memory of his homeland would not go away. While his head was telling him he was better off in America, his heart was saying something quite different. Eventually he moved back to London.

A core theme of the Christian faith is that this world is not our true homeland. We have been placed here for a reason, and there are things for us to do. But as Cyprian of Carthage (a Christian bishop executed in 258 by the Roman authorities for his faith) declared, 'paradise is our native land'. Or as Paul reminds the Christians in the Roman colony of Philippi, 'Our citizenship is in heaven' (Philippians 3.20). We are journeying through this land, doing what we can to make it a better place, while at the same time knowing that we belong in another country. Home is where the heart is; and our hearts long to be with God.

Suppose that we were made to discover and love God, and that there is some kind of 'homing instinct' for God within us. If we were indeed created for another world, how would this play out in the real world of human experience? We could expect – indeed *predict* – a sense of agitation, reflecting the fact that we are not where we really belong. Augustine of Hippo (354–430) expressed this theme well in a prayer written around the year 400: 'You have made us for yourself, and our heart is restless until it finds its rest in you.'[14] If nothing in this world really satisfies us, it is because deep down we know that our heart's desire is anchored elsewhere.

This sense of yearning for something that seems to lie beyond the frontiers of human experience is a constant theme in western literature. German Romantic writers spoke of *Sehnsucht*, described by the poet Matthew Arnold (1822–88) as a 'wistful, soft, tearful longing'. The Russian novelist Fyodor

Dostoyevsky (1821–81) expressed 'a nostalgic yearning, bordering at times on unendurably poignant sorrow' that he experienced in 'the dreams of my heart and in the reveries of my soul', pointing to something of immense significance beyond the borders of human experience.[15] And in 1916 Bertrand Russell (1872–1970), one of the most articulate and influential British atheist writers of the twentieth century, wrote:

> The centre of me is always and eternally a terrible pain . . . a searching for something beyond what the world contains, something transfigured and infinite – the beatific vision, God – I do not find it, I do not think it is to be found – but the love of it is my life . . . it is the actual spring of life within me.[16]

Russell's daughter, Katharine Tait, recalled that he was contemptuous of organized religion, dismissing its ideas mainly because he disliked those who held them. Yet Tait took the view that her father's life was really a search for God. 'Somewhere at the back of my father's mind, at the bottom of his heart, in the depths of his soul, there was an empty space that had once been filled by God, and he never found anything else to put in it.'[17] Russell was now haunted by a 'ghost-like feeling of not belonging in this world'.

This is something many of us experience – a deep sense that we belong elsewhere. Surely there is something *better*; something *more* than what we know? Does thinking this suggest that we are the victims of a meaningless delusion? Or might it be a clue to the meaning of our lives, and our place in the greater scheme of things?

For some helpful reflections on this subject, let's turn again to C. S. Lewis, who was aware of a feeling of divine restlessness throughout the years before his conversion to Christianity. Lewis observes that most people yearn for something, only to find their hopes dashed and frustrated when they actually attain it. 'There was something we grasped at, in that first moment of longing, which just fades away in the reality.'[18]

It's a concept that the novelist Virginia Woolf (1882–1941) understood. She wrote of what she called her 'moments of being' – short, stabbing instances of insight, which seemed to her to reveal 'some real thing behind appearances'.[19] These transitory and rare 'moments' convinced her that there were hidden webs of meaning and connectedness behind the world she knew. Yet she could never enter this hidden world; it always seemed to retreat from her as she approached its door.

You too may have felt that you were on the threshold of something deep and significant, only to find entry barred as the moment of insight faded away. The deep sense that there is 'something there' haunts us, though hardened rationalists may dismiss it as superstitious nonsense.

Why is it so difficult to grasp the elusive significance of this kind of experience? Lewis suggests that there are three possible answers. First, because we are looking for meaning in the wrong place. Second, because there is actually no meaning to be found. But third, and more helpfully, we could regard these earthly longings as 'a kind of copy, or echo, or mirage' of our true desires. They are 'arrows of joy', shot from our true homeland, designed to wake us from our spiritual slumber. No earthly pleasures could satisfy our yearning for more – and neither are they meant to. Their purpose is to arouse us, to suggest that there is something real to be found, and to make us restless so that we search for its source. 'Sometimes wishing is the wings the truth comes on. Sometimes the truth is what sets us wishing for it.'[20]

Personal relationships can create a bitter-sweet longing for something more significant – something that *comes through* the relationship, but is not actually *in* that relationship. It's a theme that recurs again and again in great literature. Evelyn Waugh's famous novel *Brideshead Revisited* (1945) conveys the frustration many of us will encounter (to some degree at least) through the experiences of the novel's central figure – the world-weary Captain Charles Ryder. At the beginning of his 'sacred and profane memories', he is a student 'in search of love'; by the end, he is 'homeless, childless, middle-aged and loveless', musing on how his quests seem doomed to fail to find their object.

Pleasure, beauty, personal relationships: all seem to promise so much, and yet when we try to grasp them, we find that what we are seeking is not located in these things at all. Lewis suggests that we gradually come to realize, as he did, that, 'If I find in myself a desire which no experience in this world can satisfy, the most probable explanation is that I was made for another world.'[21] Just as physical hunger points to a real need that can be met through food, so spiritual hunger corresponds to an equally real need that can be met through God.

This does not, of course, prove that Christianity is true. Nor does it prove that there is a God. But that's not Lewis's point. His argument is that our experience chimes in with what the theory suggests. The 'big picture' is able to fit it in and make sense of it.

Let's look at how the Christian big picture is able to fit in a second aspect of human experience.

A sense of moral obligation

It is very difficult to be a normal human being and not think that some actions really are wrong and some really are right.

But there is a problem with this. For if Richard Dawkins is correct in believing that 'good' is just something we invent, then we have to face up to the deeply disturbing fact that, as the American philosopher Richard Rorty (1931–2007) put it, 'there is nothing deep down inside us except what we have put there ourselves'.[22] If we decide what's right, we pretty much have to decide what's wrong. If there is no such thing as absolute truth, we can choose what we want to be true, and questions of morality are reduced to a matter of taste.

Rorty was profoundly uncomfortable with his own conclusions, not unnaturally. For what could he say when 'torturers violate the innocent' if there was no authority beyond human culture to be invoked? Nonetheless, he insisted, that was just the way things were. His colleagues and students disagreed, and regularly challenged him on the point. In the end, Rorty simply refused to discuss his views. But you can't run away from this evasion of issues.

Suppose right and wrong are just matters of personal choice – things that we have invented. What if preferring liberty to oppression is like preferring chocolate to vanilla ice cream – a matter of personal inclination? What, then, if we see people doing something we believe to be profoundly misguided, even though those doing it believe it to be right? Nazi Germany seems to have thought it was perfectly acceptable to exterminate Jews. Fortunately, others thought this was reprehensible. Moral relativism (the idea that there are no objective moral values to judge things by) implodes, finding itself unable to provide a secure basis for its fundamental convictions. 'This is good' becomes reduced to 'I like this' or 'my friends and I like this'. Justice then becomes a matter of power and influence, in which the ideas of interest groups are enforced.

It's an important point. Even the most hardened moral relativist has problems defending the view that you do what you like. Nobody really takes that view seriously. As Lewis points out, we are all aware of something 'higher' than us – a norm to which people appeal, and which they expect others to observe; a 'real law which we did not invent, and which we know we ought to obey'.[23]

And it's not just about personal issues. The Italian dictator Benito Mussolini (1883–1945) realized that the moral relativism of the 1920s made it possible for him to establish a fascist state in Italy. Since the wisdom of that age was that 'all ideologies are of equal value', in that they are all 'mere fictions', then it didn't matter what you believed. Everyone was free to 'create their own ideology, and to attempt to enforce it with all the energy of which they are capable'.[24] Mussolini drew the conclusion that his fascist ideology would triumph in Italy, since the cultural outlook of the age pulled out the rug from under any serious intellectual criticism of his ideas. And that's what happened.

Yet there is a massive disconnection between this way of thinking and the deepest intuitions of the human heart. If there is no 'natural justice' built into the structure of the universe, what's to stop power groups within society imposing their own ideas about what is right and wrong? And how can we resist this, if there is nothing beyond us that holds these people to account for their ideas and what they do with them?

Many secular ethical thinkers, such as the Anglo-Irish philosopher Iris Murdoch (1919–99), have recognized the implications of this. Murdoch argued that we are compelled to believe that, 'as moral beings, we are immersed in a reality which transcends us and that moral progress consists in awareness of this reality and submission to its purposes'.[25] Plato believed that human notions of justice were ultimately echoes of a transcendent notion of justice, lying beyond human manipulation or control. For Murdoch, belief in a transcendent idea of justice was the only way of avoiding reducing 'right' and 'wrong' to the arbitrary views of those who were powerful in society. It can't be right that the powerful call the shots, and fix the rules so that they win every time.

That was the conclusion the poet W. H. Auden (1907–73) reached in 1939 – the year after his famous 'Stop all the clocks' poem was published – following his arrival in New York. Auden had lost his religious faith in the early 1920s, adopting instead a vague left-wing outlook that emphasized the fundamental goodness of human nature and the ability of human reason to resolve crises. Shortly after the outbreak of the Second World War in Europe, he went to a movie theatre in a German-American district of Manhattan and watched a newsreel depicting the Nazi attack on Poland. He was appalled when 'quite ordinary, supposedly harmless Germans' in the audience began shouting 'Kill the Poles!'[26]

Shocked, Auden realized that he could no longer believe that human nature was good. Yet if he was to say that such things were absolutely evil, he had to have some absolute standard by which he could defend this judgement. As the significance of this sank in, he realized that his liberalism was self-defeating: 'The whole trend of liberal thought has been to undermine faith in the absolute.' Auden's return to faith in God was triggered by his realization of the importance of the 'absolute', and the ability of the Christian 'big picture' to incorporate and defend it.

Auden and many others came to see that the Christian way of thinking helps us make sense of these kinds of dilemmas and move towards a solution. God is the ultimate foundation and safeguard of justice, no matter how badly humans fail to grasp and implement this. Our deep sense of moral obligation is a fingerprint of God, a reflection of God's vision for a renewed creation, and an invitation to us to help make this world a better place. Once again, this is not about proving that Christianity is true. Rather, it is another example of how well the Christian intellectual framework seems to correspond with what we experience in our lives, and with the deepest intuitions of our hearts.

Expanding our vision

Throughout this chapter, we have been exploring the idea that Christianity enables us to see the big picture; it expands our vision of life to allow us to appreciate the depths of reality, rather than limiting our vision to the very restricted realm of what we can 'prove'. It is one of the most assured results of philosophy that reason has its limits, as do logic and science. We have seen that all three can be extraordinarily useful in helping us avoid making mistakes. But knowing that you cannot draw a triangle with six sides does not go very far towards answering the really important questions about life. It won't help us find, let alone grasp, the truth, beauty and goodness that lie at the heart of a meaningful life.

As we touched on earlier, everywhere around us there are hints and clues of a world beyond the frontiers of reason that we are invited to explore and inhabit. We may hear snatches of its music in the quiet moments of life. Or sense its fragrance wafted towards us by a gentle breeze on a cool evening. Or hear stories of others who have discovered this land, and are ready to share their adventures. All these 'signals of transcendence' encourage us to believe that there is more to existence than our everyday experience. As G. K. Chesterton pointed out, the human imagination reaches beyond the limits of reason. 'Every true artist', he argued, feels 'that he is touching transcendental truths; that his images are shadows of things seen through the veil.'[27]

Imagine someone strolling up and down a long, sandy island beach. One day, as he walks along the shoreline, he notices something that has been washed up by the tide. It is a strange plant, like nothing he has seen before. He shakes his head, puzzled. Where has this come from? Nothing similar grows on his island. Then he realizes its significance. It has come from another land – a land beyond his horizon, brought there by the ocean currents. The world turns out to be bigger than he realized.

Having aroused our suspicions that there is more to life than the bleak landscape of modern secularism, these signals of transcendence, or echoes of a divine voice, don't prove anything in and of themselves. But they do make a lot of sense when seen within the context of the Christian big picture.

Yet the God who planted these clues in the created order does not hang around, waiting for us to notice him. God chooses both to speak to us, and to come and find us. Some philosophers assert that reason leads only to the idea of God as some kind of first principle of the universe. Yet we must gently insist that God cannot be limited by reason in this way. There is no good philosophical reason for not believing in a God who speaks – who, in some sense of the word, wants to be *known*. The Christian vision of God does not contradict reason; it simply expands and enriches it, transcending the limitations of the slick and superficial rationalism that so many seem to take for granted.

To explore this further, let's use a familiar analogy, found in the writings of the classic Greek philosopher Plato. Plato asks us to imagine a group of people, trapped all their lives in an underground cave.[28] A fire is burning, casting flickering shadows on the cave's walls. These people don't know any other world. The cave is the only reality they have ever experienced. They have nothing to compare it with. As far as they are concerned, this is the world in its totality. Yet the reader knows – and is meant to know – that there is so much more awaiting their discovery.

I remember very well the first time I ever read this passage in Plato. I was in my final year at high school, waiting to go up to Oxford to study the natural sciences in depth. I felt as if I were poised on the brink of a new and wonderful world that would confirm my youthful atheism and give it new intellectual resilience. As I read Plato's analogy, the hard-nosed rationalist within me smiled condescendingly. Typical escapist superstition! What you see is what you get, and that's the end of the matter. But a still, small voice whispered words of doubt. What if this world is only part of the picture? What if this world is only a shadowland? What if there is something more wonderful beyond it?

Had I come across the writings of C. S. Lewis at that stage, I would have known that he once experienced the same dilemma, as the imaginative deficiency of his youthful atheism began to dawn on him. Yet even without reading Lewis, a seed of uncertainty had been planted within my intransigent atheist mindset. I could not have known then, but within a year, my doubts would grow to the point where they overwhelmed me and led me to rediscover Christianity.

Suppose we take Plato's analogy a stage further and ask the crucial question: how could the people in the cave become aware that reality was much bigger than their cramped and dingy cavern? They know only a dark, smoky world; how could they discover that beyond it lies a bright, brilliant and clear land of fresh breezes, intoxicating fragrances, rich colours and lush landscapes?

There might be clues within the cave to suggest the existence of a world beyond its damp and dark walls. When the wind blew in the right direction, our subterranean inhabitants might catch the scent of a distant flower, or hear the murmur of a mountain stream. They might find inexplicable drawings etched on its walls of things they had never seen.

There is another possibility. What if someone from outside were to enter the cave? What if this person were to explain what lay beyond and offered to take them there? In the end, the people in the cave would have to make a decision: will we trust this stranger, or not? Will we allow him to lead us out of the familiar place we have always known to a new and mysterious world?

These themes are explored in the Gospel accounts of the ministry of Jesus of Nazareth in the New Testament. Who is this person? Is he to be trusted? Is there a world beyond the one we know, and can Jesus of Nazareth tell us anything about it? Or lead us into it? Is he just a respectable religious teacher, with a few useful tips about living a good life? Or is he the one who is able to change everything, bring healing to those who are broken and wounded, and give us hope in the face of death?

We shall examine these themes in more detail in later volumes. For the meantime, our focus is on the 'big picture' – a vision of reality that the Christian faith asks us to trust, invites us to enter and encourages us to unpack and savour. We've looked at some aspects of this theme in this present chapter. In the next, we will focus in turn on three models or images that will help us explore the big picture further.

2

The map, the lens and the light: making sense of things

———◆◆———

Discovering new things always adds interest to life. A colleague of mine who had read *Moby Dick* was inspired by Herman Melville's remark about having an 'everlasting itch for things remote'. He began travelling to distant parts of the world: one year he visited the highlands of Vietnam; the next, he rode the railways of Patagonia. He was driven by an unquenchable desire to see new things, to 'sail forbidden seas, and land on barbarous coasts', as Melville had before him.

But there's another voyage of discovery we can make, and this, as the French novelist Marcel Proust (1871–1922) once remarked, 'does not consist in searching for new landscapes, but in seeing them with new eyes'. When we do this, the familiar takes on new meaning; the ordinary becomes special. Our eyes need to be opened and our sight healed, so that we can perceive things as they really are.

Seeing things through new eyes

To help explain this important point, let me tell the tale of a mysterious block of stone discovered in Canford School in Dorset. The school was founded in 1923 when an old country manor house was purchased and renovated for educational use. The house had previously been owned by Sir Henry Layard (1818–94), a prominent Victorian archaeologist who had spent much of his time excavating ancient sites in Mesopotamia, and was credited with the discovery of the 'lost' city of Nineveh in 1845. The builders who converted the house into a school found some large blocks of stone in one of the rooms. The school management had no idea what to do with them. For a while, one of them was used to prop up the school's dartboard. Eventually, it was moved to the school's 'tuck shop', which sold drinks and confectionery to students.

In 1994 John Russell, a professor of art history at Columbia University, who was researching a book about Layard, visited Canford School.[1] While exploring the premises, he noticed this slab of stone close to the drinks machine and pizza counter. Russell's curiosity was aroused. After a trip to the British Museum in London, he realized that it was a 3,000-year-old carved panel that Layard had brought back to England from the throne room of the Assyrian King Assurnasirpal II (883–859 BC). It was sold at auction at Christie's later that year for a record $11.8 million.

When Russell first saw the stone, he assumed that he was looking at a cheap plaster copy of an ancient Assyrian carving. Then his eyes were opened and he realized what the stone really was. He discerned its true significance. As a result, the way the object was understood and valued changed radically. What was once seen as a useless lump of rock was now recognized as an important historical relic, worth nearly $12 million.

The key point is that the stone *was seen with new eyes*. Russell displayed what the philosopher Iris Murdoch called 'attentiveness' – a careful, principled, committed attempt to perceive things as they really are, rather than as they merely appear to be. We may approach an object with a set of assumptions, then discover as we look at it that these do not tie in very well with what we are actually observing. So we begin to look for another way of seeing that fits better.

It's an idea that is familiar to scientists. The philosopher of science N. R. Hanson (1924–67) pointed out that we all look at the world through 'theoretical spectacles', whether we realize this or not. What kind of spectacles might bring things into sharpest focus? The Harvard psychologist William James (1842–1910) declared that religious faith is basically 'faith in the existence of an unseen order of some kind in which the riddles of the natural order may be found and explained'.[2] To find that 'unseen order' is to open up a new way of looking at things, which allows us to see them differently. This way is not grounded in human wisdom, but rooted ultimately in the reality of God.

It's a point that is familiar to us from the New Testament. When Paul urges his readers to 'be transformed by the renewing of your minds' (Romans 12.2), he is asking us to put on Christian spectacles and see the world afresh. The New Testament uses many images to make it clear that the Christian faith brings about a new way of envisaging the world. My three favourites are these: our sight is healed; our eyes are opened; a veil is removed.

One of the things I've noticed as I get older is how other people help me to see things more clearly. They point out things I've missed. And sometimes, they have to correct me when I get things wrong. That's why it's so important that Christianity is a corporate rather than an individual faith. Others help us explore its landscape. C. S. Lewis found that his Christian faith was significantly deepened by the insights of friends such as J. R. R. Tolkien and Charles Williams. What others saw helped Lewis to see further.

> My own eyes are not enough for me, I will see through those of others . . . In reading great literature, I become a thousand men and yet remain myself. Like the night sky in the Greek poem, I see with a myriad eyes, but it is still I who see.[3]

My favourite description of exploring the landscape of faith comes from the pen of Evelyn Waugh, whose *Brideshead Revisited* we discussed earlier. After his sudden conversion to Christianity in 1930, Waugh wrote to a friend describing how his new faith allowed him to see things clearly for the first time:

> Conversion is like stepping across the chimney piece out of a Looking-Glass world, where everything is an absurd caricature, into the real world God made; and then begins the delicious process of exploring it limitlessly.[4]

Before coming to faith, Waugh saw only a distorted world of smoke and mirrors; after his conversion, he saw things as they really were. He began to explore this new landscape with excitement, enthusiasm and wonder, as his later writings make clear.

But where do we start? How do we find our way to this world's main features? One answer is especially helpful in making sense of Christian belief. If you want to explore a landscape, you need a map.

The map: the landscape of faith

As every explorer will tell you, a good map is essential to help you get your bearings. Whether you're traversing a mountain range or simply trying to get home, a map will reveal the way to go (if you know how to read it). It will show you the big picture of the landscape, so you can work out where you are, or what you're looking for. Then you will begin to notice some of the features. Let's linger on this thought for a moment.

Recently, when I was leading a small group at a conference at Oxford, dealing with the 'imaginative appeal of faith', I asked the dozen or so people in my group to tell me what they found so valuable about their faith. For some, it was the stability it brought to their lives; for others, it was knowing God's presence, even in life's darker moments. A few spoke warmly of the sense of being loved; others of the way faith helped them make sense of things. They all believed in the same 'big picture'; yet each found one aspect of that picture especially powerful.

What was really interesting, however, was the way that people reacted to what others were saying. Those who valued the Christian emphasis on being loved by God realized that there was more for them to discover – such as how faith might help them make sense of things. Even though everyone found their faith helpful and meaningful, they realized that there was more to it than they had appreciated.

What drew me to Christianity as a young man was its ability to make sense of things. In one respect, my conversion was very intellectual. Yet as I grew older, I began to appreciate other aspects of my faith – such as its ethical vision, its strong sense of purpose in life, its ability to secure personal identity, and its powerful appeal to the imagination. All these features (to continue our map illustration) were already there; I simply discovered them.

Now maps are not the same as a landscape. Think of somewhere special you've visited – perhaps a Caribbean island, an Umbrian landscape, or the mountains and forests of California. Can you remember what it was like to experience its natural beauty? Now imagine this special place on a map. How does that two-dimensional representation compare with the three-dimensional reality? Poorly, I expect! A map cannot convey the vibrant colours, the rich textures and the subtle fragrances of a glorious landscape. A diagram on a piece of paper is never going to do justice to the beauty and majesty of the natural world. *But it's not meant to.* It's there to help you explore and discover, and find your way to where you want to be.

The map we find in the creeds is there to help us explore the landscape of faith and to find our way back home. It's a map that distils the core themes of the Bible, disclosing a glorious, loving and righteous God, who creates a world that goes wrong, and then acts graciously and wondrously in order to renew and redirect it, before finally bringing it to its fulfilment. And we ourselves are an integral part of this story that reveals our true purpose, meaning and value – who we are, what is wrong, what God proposes to do about this, and what we must do in response.

Christian beliefs are not like a set of individual, unrelated ideas. They are held together by the compelling and persuasive vision of reality that is made possible by the gospel. We see a breathtaking landscape, and marvel at its beauty; then we move on to take in its features. To understand the beliefs, we must first catch the vision. To make sense of the snapshots, we need to take in the panorama. We can think of creeds as maps that help us understand how Christian beliefs inter-connect – just as maps show us how towns and cities are interconnected by roads.

We'll be looking at these creeds in more detail later in this volume, and finding out how this 'map of faith' came into being. Yet the analogy of a map is only one way of helping us understand what Christian beliefs are all about. Let's move on and look at another.

The lens: bringing reality into focus

Imagine that you are walking along a sandy beach on a beautiful day. Ahead of you is a deep blue ocean, stretching as far as you can see into the distance. As you look, you catch a glimpse of something moving. You have a small telescope with you. You reach for it, and point it out to sea. To begin with everything is blurred, but as you adjust the lens, things suddenly become sharp and clear. You can see a yacht shimmering in the distance; you can even make out individual crew members moving around on its deck.

Christianity is about bringing things into focus. For many people, life seems to have no meaning. It appears to be random, meaningless and chaotic, without any underlying order or significance. We are born. We die. And what lies in between is nothing but 'a tale told by an idiot, full of sound and fury, signifying nothing'.[5] But perhaps there are other ways of reflecting on things. Perhaps they seem meaningless because they are out of focus? Or because we have blurred vision? What if there is a way of looking at things that allows us to see more clearly?

When I was young, it was a great treat to go to the fairground that passed through my home town about once a year. I retain a vivid memory of its hall of mirrors. As I walked past these mirrors, I would see a figure that I recognized as myself – yet distorted. Sometimes I would be fat, sometimes thin; sometimes tall, sometimes squat. I was misshapen. But was this really the way I was, or just the way I seemed to be? What was the caricature, and what the reality?

Christianity gives us a lens through which we can see ourselves and our world for what they really are. One of the finest statements of this principle is found in the poetry of George Herbert (1593–1633), especially in these lines:

> A man that looks on glass,
> On it may stay his eye;
> Or if he pleaseth, through it pass,
> And then the heav'n espy.[6]

Herbert was writing in the early seventeenth century, when two inventions that made use of lenses – often referred to as 'glasses' at this time – were transforming human appreciation of the natural world. He draws a clear distinction between the different modes of viewing these allow: *looking at*, and *looking through*. You can look at a window or a telescope. Or you can look through them, and find yourself in a new world.

In Herbert's day, the microscope allowed a new wealth of detail to be seen in the petals of flowers and the wings of butterflies, while the telescope revealed the moons of the planet Jupiter and the mass of stars that made up the Milky Way. Both instruments allowed people to view things that had always been there but had not previously been evident, because they lay beyond the frontiers of human sight. We could not see them, because our eyes were not good enough. An expansion of vision was needed to open up these new worlds.

Herbert's comments, however, are primarily about theology and concern the purpose and place of Christian beliefs. He helps us understand that we can approach beliefs in two ways. First, we can look *at* them, an approach found in many traditional textbooks of theology, which set out each individual belief and allow its distinct themes to be appreciated. But second, we can look *through* them, as if they were a telescope enabling us to 'espy heaven' – and enjoy an enriched view of reality, resulting from a heightened ability to discern what is really there.

Embracing Christianity's 'bigger picture' helps us realize that each of us, being created in God's image, matters profoundly; and that status and wealth mean nothing compared to the riches of knowing God. As Thomas à Kempis (*c*.1380–1471) pointed out in his spiritual classic *The Imitation of Christ*, when it was seen in perspective, 'the glory of the world fades away'.

Yet some people *choose* to keep seeing the world through a distorting mirror. Iris Murdoch was aware of the unsettling fact that human beings often find reality somewhat uncomfortable, and prefer to invent ways of looking at the world that are less inconvenient. As a result, 'by opening our eyes we do not necessarily see what confronts us'. Why not? Because we shield ourselves from reality by 'fabricating an anxious, usually self-preoccupied, often falsifying *veil* which partially conceals the world'.[7] We sometimes put on a set of rose-tinted spectacles that allows us to pretend that everything is fine. The true meaning of things can be too disturbing for comfort.

Looking at things through a Christian lens, on the other hand, brings our true situation into focus, enabling us to realize that we cannot go on as we are. It brings home to us that we are sinful. We're like people who have fallen into a pit and can't get out. We need someone to rescue us. To use a medical analogy: the Christian framework of meaning acts as a diagnostic tool, showing us that something is wrong with us, and telling us the treatment that is needed if we are to be cured. We are liberated from the delusion that all is well, and shown what needs to be done if things are to be put right.

The light: illuminating the shadowlands

The Christian way of thinking illuminates the world, enabling us to see things more clearly, even in the shadowlands of this life. Imagine you are standing on a hilltop, overlooking a vast landscape. It is dark, and you are facing west. Behind you, the sun begins to rise. Gradually, the shadows disappear, and the countryside lights up. Everything that is illuminated below you was already there a few hours ago. But only now can you see the detail. The coming of the light brings discernment and vision.

This idea has a rich history within the Christian tradition. 'The Lord is my light and my salvation' (Psalm 27.1). 'Your word is a lamp to my feet and a light to my path' (Psalm 119.105). One of the central points made by Christian theologians is that light shows up things as they really are, dispelling illusions. Illumination allows a reality check, forcing us to confront what are at times some awkward truths.

In my second year at Oxford University, I was given a room in one of the oldest parts of Wadham College. At night, the room looked very elegant. But in the morning, as the sunlight streamed in through the windows, it showed up the cracks in the walls, the decaying wallpaper and the tatty old carpet. I often thought it would be more pleasant to live in the half-light and not have to face up to the faded grandeur around me.

Being forced to confront reality has a much darker side. Many of us who have read about the Nazi Holocaust during the Second World War are shocked by the brutality, bloodshed and barbarism of extermination camps like Auschwitz. Yet one of the most distressing things about these death camps is what they tell us about ourselves. Although some atheists improbably suggest that God caused the Holocaust, the harsh reality is that this event was planned and perpetrated by human beings. It is a difficult problem for secular rationalists, who make human beings the 'measure of all things' (Alexander Pope), to confront the reality that these same human beings can be utterly barbaric. That realization, as we saw earlier, caused W. H. Auden to abandon his naive belief in human goodness, and realign himself towards God.

What Auden and countless others discovered is that the Christian way of looking at human nature is far more realistic. This approach holds that we are, first, created in the 'image of God' and, second, sinful. We find ourselves excited and inspired by the vision of God, which draws us upwards; yet we also find ourselves pulled down by the frailty and fallenness of human nature. It is a familiar dilemma, famously articulated by Paul: 'I do not do the good I want, but the evil I do not want is what I do' (Romans 7.19).

So from a Christian perspective, we must recognize that while human beings are capable of greater things than most political systems or philosophies allow, we are equally capable of failing to live up to our potential. Christian theology gives us a critical lens through which to view our complex motivations and mixed agendas: we bear God's image yet we are sinful; we are capable of good yet capable of evil; our culture and history are characterized by aspirations to greatness and goodness on the one hand, and the practice of oppression and violence on the other.

This way of seeing ourselves is unsettling for those who want to enthrone humanity. The easiest way of dealing with an uncomfortable truth is to deny it or try to sweep it under the carpet. But it just won't go away. Any 'big picture' of reality has to be able to explain the profound moral ambiguity of human nature. Indeed, many are drawn to the understanding Christianity offers because it faces up to the fact that human beings are capable of intentionally doing evil. We shall have more to say about this in a later volume. The important point is that we need a big picture that can be trusted – one that can cope with the moral complexity of reality.

For one of the best explorations of how Christianity offers a trustworthy account of reality, we turn again to C. S. Lewis. 'I believe in Christianity as I believe that the Sun has risen, not only because I see it, but because by it, I see everything else.'[8] This powerful statement invites us to judge Christianity by its capacity to make sense of the world. The more a worldview can explain, the more likely it is to be true. Christianity's success or failure in this area is one reason why people may or may not believe it is worth embracing.

G. K. Chesterton had no doubt that Christianity made sense of things, and this played a key role in his return to faith. Chesterton's spiritual journey took a decisive turn in 1903, when he published a newspaper article explaining why he and many others now regarded Christianity with intense intellectual solemnity.[9] 'We have returned to it because it is an intelligible picture of the world.'

Chesterton realized that testing a theory meant checking it out against observation. 'The best way to see if a coat fits a man is not to measure both of them, but to try it on.' Let Chesterton himself explain what he has in mind.

> Numbers of us have returned to this belief; and we have returned to it, not because of this argument or that argument, but because the theory, when it is adopted, works out everywhere; because the coat, when it is tried on, fits in every crease . . . We put on the theory, like a magic hat, and history becomes translucent like a house of glass.

Chesterton's argument here reinforces a point we keep returning to: that Christianity offers a big picture, and it is this vision of reality as a whole – rather than any of its individual components – that proves so compelling. Individual observations of nature do not 'prove' Christianity to be true; rather, Christianity validates itself by its ability to make sense of those observations. 'The phenomenon does not prove religion, but religion explains the phenomenon.'

For Chesterton, a good theory is to be judged by the amount of illumination it offers, and its capacity to accommodate what we see in the world around us and experience within us. 'With this idea once inside our heads, a million things become transparent as if a lamp were lit behind them.' Much the same point was made by the French philosopher and social activist Simone Weil (1909–43), who discovered the Christian faith relatively late in her short life. She was drawn to its winsome way of illuminating life's enigmas:

If I light an electric torch at night out of doors I don't judge its power by looking at the bulb, but by seeing how many objects it lights up. . . . The value of a religious or, more generally, a spiritual way of life is appreciated by the amount of illumination thrown upon the things of this world.[10]

Yet though the Christian faith illuminates the world around us, some shadowlands remain. What was dark may become clearer, but everything is not yet made plain. As Paul points out: 'For now, we see in a mirror, dimly' (1 Corinthians 13.12). His imagery speaks of a blurred, fuzzy or even distorted view of things that does not show how they really are. The landscape of faith includes distant and dim borderlands, not fully illuminated by the light of the sun.

So while the Christian faith allows us to see further than we otherwise could, it reminds us that there are still limits to our sight. Faith trusts that God journeys with us, even when we are bewildered and perplexed. We may not perceive God in everything, but God sees us, wherever we are. 'If I take the wings of the morning and settle at the farthest limits of the sea, even there your hand shall lead me, and your right hand shall hold me fast' (Psalm 139.9–10). God's presence and care do not depend on our discernment or comprehension: God is with us, even when sight or reason fails.

3

Words and stories: discovering the deeper significance of faith

Christianity helps us make sense of things. It allows us to look at the world through new eyes and see it in a different way. Of course, we cannot expect *everything* to come into focus, or hope that *all* the shadowlands will be illuminated. But somehow it is possible to cope better with uncertainties and difficulties because we are gaining a sense of direction and purpose for our lives. The creeds give us a framework for going further and deeper into our faith. Yet many find their words and phrases inadequate, if not occasionally baffling.

When words aren't good enough

Our present chapter focuses on this problem. We have to use words to refer to life's deepest intuitions, most important moments and greatest excitements – whether falling in love or discovering God – but often find that those words just aren't good enough to convey the meaning or the intensity of our thoughts. Words let us down when we try to write a letter expressing our sadness at the death of a friend to his surviving relatives, or tell someone how much they mean to us, or how they have helped us during a dark time. Of course, poetry can sometimes be helpful in expressing what seems inexpressible to us, but for the most part, we struggle to find words good enough to do the job. The Austrian philosopher Ludwig Wittgenstein (1889–1951) famously pointed out that it was impossible to convey the aroma of freshly ground coffee in words.

And the problem is not limited to coffee or the kind of personal experiences mentioned above. Imagine that you are standing on a mountain ridge in the Alps. Below you, spread out like a tapestry, is a beautiful landscape, stretching into the far distance. Woods, streams, fields, villages are all lit by the gentle radiance of a late afternoon sun. How would you describe this vista to someone back home?

The fact is, you can't. It is impossible to express something so wonderful in words – 'I saw a lovely view' doesn't even come close! Even as you struggle, you realize that you simply don't have the vocabulary to communicate the glory of the experience. There is always going to be a significant gap between a word and the reality to which it points. You could tell your friend about a wood you saw in the distance from the mountaintop; but the little word 'wood' will not evoke the memory of a green mass of trees, dappled leaves shimmering in the sunlight, or your emotional reaction to this scene of beauty.

Of course, you could draw a map to show the positions of the various elements – where the woods are in relation to the mountains, the streams in relation to the villages, and so on. But as we saw in the last chapter, a map is merely a two-dimensional rendering of a three-dimensional landscape, and the things that moved you to wonder and delight – the beautiful view, the cool wind, the fragrance of flowers and resin, the distant tinkling of cowbells as the herds wander around seeking the best pastures – are hardly going to be conveyed to your friend through some scribbling on a piece of paper.

No wonder so many abandon words and reach for a camera. Yet even photographs fall short. To experience the wonder of an Alpine landscape, or a tropical island surrounded by an azure sea, you need to go there yourself. Words and images can never represent reality in all its fullness.

However, we have to use words; we simply don't have a choice. And the fact is that although words have limitations, they also have power. Words can change everything.

Think of a man in debt for more than everything he owns, facing bankruptcy and ruin, who gets an urgent message from his accountant: 'The debt has been cancelled'. Think of an ageing couple whose only son has been kidnapped in the Middle East and threatened with death. They are called by a national newspaper with the dramatic news: 'Your son is being released'. Or imagine a young woman who feels she is drowning in emptiness and loneliness. The man she secretly adores visits unexpectedly and tells her: 'I love you'.

Here, words are tokens of transforming news – of developments that change everything. In a similar way, while the verbal formulae we call 'Christian beliefs' can seem a little wooden and lacklustre, they express matters that run deep and speak to the heart as well as the mind. Declarations such as 'I believe in God' may seem like cool, dispassionate and disinterested statements, but the truth is much more complex and interesting than that.

Wittgenstein (of the coffee example above) does more than point out the limits of words in everyday life. He also reminds us that if we want to know what words *really* mean, we ought to listen to how they are used. 'Words have meaning only in the stream of life.'[1] Dictionary definitions let us down; we need to allow people to explain to us what certain ideas convey to them, and how this affects their everyday experience. This is especially true of the Christian use of the word 'faith'.

Let's listen to four very different people expressing their understanding of the opening words of the creed – 'I believe in God'. I asked them to try and put into words what their faith in God meant to them. First, we hear from a woman in the legal profession, who has been a Christian for about 20 years.

> I used to think that life was meaningless, and that my longing for truth and beauty was just a pointless delusion. Then I discovered my heart's desire, and everything was changed. I found the peace that I so earnestly desired. And the name of my heart's desire was God.

The second to speak was a retired schoolteacher who has been a Christian all his life, and found faith a great consolation in his later years. His comments were brief and to the point.

> Without God my life would be bleak and empty.

The third person who tried to express her faith was a student, who had always seen herself as a Christian but had begun to think about things more deeply while at university.

> I found that the Bible tells us the truth and that there is a God who loves us. God's words are my strength and my rock.

The fourth witness was a local businessman, with a very down-to-earth approach to life.

My walk of faith is about having a true and deep relationship with God and realizing how much he loves me, despite my failures.

In one way, these four accounts of faith are very different. Christianity is a public faith but it has private dimensions, connecting up with the individual identity and concerns of each person. For some, faith gives stability to life; for others, faith is about being loved and valued; for yet others, faith is about being able to make sense of things. There are many diverse but complementary interpretations of faith making up its rich landscape.

It isn't easy, though, to sum up what faith means to you in mere words. Words may not seem capable of expressing really deep things. However, we can still use them wisely, as signposts rather than as complete statements of what truly matters. In the end, one of the most powerful things that Christianity affirms is that the heart's desire, the meaning of life, the foundation of justice and the culmination of human hope and longing, all converge on the God who is proclaimed and disclosed by Jesus of Nazareth. And we can use words to point in this direction – to tell our own stories of faith.

In fact, recent cultural history has shown a new appreciation of the importance of stories in helping us make sense of things and allowing us to work out what is good. As we continue reflecting on how to deepen our appreciation of Christian beliefs, let's explore this point further.

The story of faith

One of the most powerful passages in the Gospels records Jesus of Nazareth's answer to the question: 'Who is my neighbour?' (Luke 10.29). Jesus answers by *telling a story* – the parable of the Good Samaritan (Luke 10.29–37). This moving and powerful tale grips our imagination and answers the question in a more memorable, powerful and challenging way than any mere dictionary definition of 'neighbour' could.

Let's ask another question: what is God like? Some will answer by reaching for a dictionary: God is the 'supreme being'. The Christian Bible, however, dispenses with dictionary definitions. Instead, it tells a story.

The story opens well, relating how God created a wonderful and beautiful world that was pronounced to be good. Soon, however, things go wrong. G. K. Chesterton identified the problem with characteristic brilliance:

> God had written, not so much a poem, but rather a play; a play he had planned as perfect, but which had necessarily been left to human actors and stage-managers, who had since made a great mess of it.[2]

So how were things to be put right? Here, the great story of faith focuses initially on an individual, then on a nation, before it expands to embrace the whole world. God calls Abraham to be the father of the people of Israel, from whom the Messiah will emerge to bring about the redemption of the world. As the 'bidding prayer' for the Service of Nine Lessons and Carols at King's College, Cambridge puts it, we should 'read and mark in Holy Scripture the tale of the loving purposes of God from the first days of our disobedience unto the glorious Redemption brought us by this Holy Child'. It is a grand epic of creation, fall, redemption and final consummation, which captures the imagination, warms the heart and enlightens our minds.

How, we might ask, does telling this story relate to statements of Christian belief? Perhaps C. S. Lewis can help us grasp the point at issue. In the 1950s, Lewis published not only *Mere Christianity* but also the much-loved children's series, 'The Chronicles of Narnia'. Many Lewis scholars argue that these works reflect the same basic themes, but where *Mere Christianity* uses reasoned argument, *The Lion, the Witch and the Wardrobe* and other volumes in the Narnia series employ narrative to explore the Christian faith. *Mere Christianity* engages the mind, but the Narnia stories appeal to the imagination.

Now it is not quite as simple as this. *Mere Christianity* appeals to the imagination at several important points. But the comparison is useful. In one work, Lewis *argues*, and asks us to accept his ideas; in the other work, he *shows*, and invites us to enter the world his story reveals.

In *The Lion, the Witch and the Wardrobe*, the four Pevensie children begin to hear stories about Narnia. But which is right? Is Narnia really the realm of the White Witch? Or is she a usurper, whose dark power needs to be broken? Is Narnia really the realm of the mysterious and noble Aslan, whose return is expected at any time? The children are forced to make decisions about which stories they can trust, and which are false. Gradually, one story emerges as supremely plausible, making sense of the evidence, and chiming in with the children's deepest intuitions: the story of Aslan. Each individual story of Narnia turns out to be part of this greater story.

Lewis crafted a fictional masterpiece, focusing on finding a principal story that makes sense of all other stories – and then embracing it, because of its power to give meaning and value to life.

Yet Lewis did not invent this Narnian story. He borrowed and adapted one that he already knew well, and had found to be true and trustworthy: the Christian story of creation, fall, redemption and final consummation. The 'grand narrative' of the Christian faith tells of how God entered into history to redeem the world. This Christian story first converges on Jesus Christ, and then radiates outwards from him. Jesus Christ is the way that God comes to us, and the way that we come to God. The story of Jesus Christ tells us who God is, and who we are.

Why does the Bible tell a story to help us grasp what we are meant to believe, and how we are meant to behave? Christian theology has given two main answers. In the first place, a narrative makes faith more accessible. God is concerned to engage with people at a level suitable for their abilities. The theme of 'divine accommodation' emphasizes the graciousness of God in choosing to use a variety of means of self-disclosure – stories, images and ideas.

The second reason is especially important for apologetics – the area of Christian thought that tries to communicate the joy and wonder of the gospel to the world. Stories have a unique power to change the way we think. They invite us to see the world in a certain way. A story that is well told can suspend disbelief, making it easier for us to consider whether what we are hearing might actually be true and trustworthy. Many readers of J. R. R. Tolkien's epic, *The Lord of the Rings*, find themselves presented with a world of such intense richness and depth that they are drawn into reflection on the deeper meaning of life.

The Story and our story

'There's a story behind that!' How often have you heard that said? I was in the study of one of my tutors in theology at

Lady Margaret Hall, Oxford University, early in 1978. After the tutorial, we stood around his bookcases as he pulled out some volumes that he thought I would enjoy reading. My eye was drawn to a book by C. S. Lewis – I cannot recall which one – in whom I was beginning to develop an interest at this time. When I asked my tutor what he made of Lewis, he laughed, picked out the book and waved it in the air. 'There's a story behind this!' he declared, and proceeded to relate it. My tutor's name was Peter Bide, and it turned out that he was the clergyman who married C. S. Lewis to Joy Davidman in an Oxford hospital in March 1957.[3] The book, for him, was a memento of that occasion. He knew its deeper meaning. And now I did as well. Bide had told me the little story that connected that book with the larger story of his life.

Let's do a thought experiment. What is there in your home that has a hidden story? That has a special meaning and significance, not immediately obvious to anyone else? What would you select?

Here's my choice. Since 1972, an old German microscope has stood on my desk. Wherever I've gone, the microscope has gone too. It was given to me back in the early 1960s by a great-uncle, who was head of pathology at the Royal Victoria Hospital, Belfast. It proved to be the gateway to a new world. As I happily explored the small plants and cells I found in pond water through its lens, I developed a love of nature that remains with me to this day.

So why do I keep this microscope? Well, first, it reminds me of a family member, who died soon after giving it to me. Second, it reminds me of my own past, enabling me to recall my youth and my hopes and aspirations for the future. And third, it acts as a symbol for what has come to be one of the major themes of my own vision of life – namely, that looking attentively at the world of nature deepens our understanding of God.

I'm sure you can think of other examples that make the same point – letters, photographs, gifts or everyday objects that, though ordinary, play a special role in connecting you with your own story.

But there is another point here. Our own stories connect up with a bigger story – with the 'grand narrative' of the Christian faith. The Christian story is not simply something that we tell; it is something of which we are part. We could think of faith as the act of becoming a participant in the 'grand narrative' and discovering the role we believe we ought to be playing in taking that greater story forward.

The creeds may be regarded as a shorthand interpretation of this grand story of faith that tells of the creation of the world, of things going wrong and then being made right again. The grand story speaks of exodus from Egypt, wandering in the wilderness and entry into a promised land. It tells of the birth of a saviour and of his death and resurrection. And finally, this grand story speaks of *us*, as we make it *our* story. To be a Christian is to allow our personal stories to be shaped and sustained by the greater Christian story.

The creeds do not tell this story *as a story*; nevertheless, they distil its significance and hit its high points. One of the finest reflections on this idea comes from the pen of Dorothy L. Sayers. In her essay, 'The Dogma is the Drama', Sayers shows how the story of Christianity conveys its theological heartbeat. (The term 'dogma' may be understood as meaning doctrine or a set of beliefs.) Most people, she suggests, 'simply cannot believe that anything so interesting, so exciting, and so dramatic can be the orthodox creed of the Church'. How could such a vivid story be transmuted into the rather dull and wooden phrases of the creed?

> It is the dogma that is the drama – not beautiful phrases, nor comforting sentiments, nor vague aspirations to loving-kindness and uplift, nor the promise of something nice after death – but the terrifying assertion that the same God who made the world lived in the world and passed through the grave and gate of death.[4]

That dramatic story, Sayers argues, holds the key to understanding what faith is all about. 'The Christian faith is the most exciting drama that ever staggered the imagination of man – and the dogma *is* the drama.'

Nonetheless, the suspicion that the creed does not really tell the story of faith as well as it might leads us to reflect further on the problems Christians experience when trying to use words to express the deepest realities of their lives.

Theory and reality

All of us want to see and understand things clearly. Yet the human mind is not well adapted to complexities. In particular, scientific reality is not always easy to visualize. When I was in my early teens, I had a pretty good idea what an atom looked like – it was similar to a miniature solar system. Right in the middle was the nucleus, consisting of neutrons and protons. The electrons orbited this nucleus, just like the planets revolve around the sun. It was all so simple.

Except it wasn't. When I began to study science in more detail at university, I realized that this was just a convenient way of picturing atoms, invented by the great physicist Ernest Rutherford (1871–1937). Atoms didn't look like this at all.

Rutherford had merely provided a useful mental image to help people visualize something invisible and intangible, and so make sense of mathematical formulae that would otherwise be hopelessly abstract.

We need pictures to help us think. That's why we have maps of landscapes and diagrams of complex pieces of machinery. They're there to allow us to make sense of what we encounter and experience. But what they represent already exists. Reality precedes its description. Nobody seriously imagines that atoms came into being only when Rutherford suggested that we think of them as tiny solar systems, or that the Alps appeared for the first time when somebody mapped them.

The same is true of Christian beliefs. They describe the deeper vision of reality that the Christian faith makes it possible to see. Our aim is to encounter that reality, and we are given a map of the landscape of faith so that we may find, inhabit and explore this new world. Some may be content with the map itself. But they would be missing out on what the map points to.

As a professional theologian, I want to insist that theories matter, and that it's important to get them right. We need to take time and trouble to make sure that our description and understanding of such matters as the character of God, or the identity and significance of Jesus of Nazareth, are as reliable and comprehensive as possible. But the reality of God is already there, in advance of our thinking. Reality precedes our beliefs about it. Our beliefs are accountable to the reality that they represent, just as the map (or those who drew it) could be said to be accountable to a landscape.

The map is not the same as the landscape, even though it may represent it reliably. Once we are in the countryside, the reduced account of reality offered by the map makes a lot more sense to us, and we can fine-tune the map in the light of what we actually encounter on the ground. But most importantly of all, we are able to flesh out the map's symbols and images because we have encountered the reality to which they point.

As every scientist knows, theories reduce reality to something manageable. They offer us a way of grasping concepts that are actually much more complex. But the price we pay is high, because reality is being scaled down to something so much less than it truly is. And there is a serious risk that in trying to scale God down to something we can handle, we lose sight of God's transcendence and glory. One of the reasons so many Christians find themselves puzzled by the doctrine of the Trinity is because they are making do with a reduced vision of God. But the real God is untameable – one who expands our minds and excites our hearts in praise and adoration.

That's why worship is such an important part of the Christian life. It reminds us that God is more than an idea – a lot more. The living and loving God sets our hearts, reasons and imaginations on fire. The author and pastor A. W. Tozer (1897–1963) was right on target when he said: 'We might be wise to follow the insight of the enraptured heart rather than the more cautious reasoning of the theological mind.'

I gradually became aware of the importance of this point when talking to some people who had embraced Christianity through attending worship. One conversation, which was particularly memorable, was with two professional people who had visited one of London's largest churches in the late 1990s. Thoroughly secular, they were curious about what drew so many people to something as hopelessly outdated as Christianity. So they decided to go to a Sunday service.

They told me that they were awed by the experience: 'These people had discovered something that we knew nothing about.' And whatever it was, my professional pair wanted to find out more. What could be so attractive and glorious that it prompted this response from the congregation? As they began to explore the Christian faith, both came to embrace the God they had seen others worship with such delight. They too sensed God's greatness. They too were moved by who God is and what God has done for us. Worship unlocked the gates of their hearts and of their minds, and their lives were never the same again.

The mystery of faith

Christian writers often speak of the importance of 'preserving the mystery of faith'. To fail to do this, they suggest, is to end up reducing Christianity to little more than sanctified common sense. We need to reflect a little more on that word 'mystery'. What does Paul mean, when he declares that 'the mystery that has been hidden throughout the ages' has now been made known (Colossians 1.26)?

When I first began to study theology back in the mid 1970s, the meaning of the word seemed obvious. A 'mystery' was some kind of riddle or puzzle. I was an avid fan of detective fiction in those days, and regularly pored over second-hand book stalls in Oxford's market, searching for Earl Stanley Gardner novels to supplement my collection. Colin Dexter's Inspector Morse series began to appear around this time, adding considerably to my delight, not least because it was set in Oxford. A mystery, as I then saw things, was a superficially baffling series of events that could be explained by some sharp detective work.

It was a good start to appreciating what Christianity was all about. As we saw back in Chapter 1, one of the many intellectual virtues of the Christian faith is that it makes sense in itself, while also making sense of what we experience in our own lives and see in the world around us. When he spoke of 'the mystery that has been hidden throughout the ages', I thought that Paul was pointing out how the coming of Jesus of Nazareth explained some of the more complicated sections of the Old Testament. But in the end, I came to see that this was only one aspect of the word 'mystery'; there was more to discover before its full richness became clear. Over a period of about ten years, I began to appreciate that the human mind cannot fully grasp the deep structures of reality. Indeed, the New Testament and Christian thinkers use the term 'mystery' to refer to the hidden depths of the Christian faith, which stretch beyond the reach of reason. In encountering the living God, we are confronted with something of overwhelming immensity.

G. K. Chesterton made this point with characteristic incision and clarity, contrasting two very different ways of thinking – that of the poet and that of the logician. Poets try to expand their minds to take in the wonder of reality; logicians try to limit the universe to what their minds can cope with.

> Poetry is sane because it floats easily in an infinite sea; reason seeks to cross the infinite sea, and so make it finite. The result is mental exhaustion . . . The poet only asks to get his head into the heavens. It is the logician who seeks to get the heavens into his head. And it is his head that splits.[5]

Christian writers down the ages have made this point, and we need to listen to them. When the poet and theologian

John Donne (1572–1631) spoke of the 'exceeding weight of glory', he was trying to express the sheer mental difficulty he experienced in putting the immensity of God into words. Divine glory leads us to worship and adoration, yet lies beyond our total comprehension.

Dorothy L. Sayers made more or less the same point in a much more homely way. Trying to get God into a verbal formula was like trying to force a large and irritated cat into a small basket. As soon as you tuck in his head, his tail comes out. Once his back paws are inside, the front paws appear again. And when you finally manage to squeeze the cat into the basket, his 'dismal wailings' make it clear that 'some essential dignity in the creature has been violated and a wrong done to its nature'.[6] If you have problems getting a cat into a basket, how are you going to squeeze God into a few words? 'To say that God is a mystery is to say that you can never nail him down. Even on Christ the nails proved ultimately ineffective.'[7]

There is always the danger that we might say, 'I can't understand this – so it's wrong', thinking that this demonstrates the irrationality of the idea when it really highlights the limits of our reason. The human imagination is so important because it compensates for the limits of reason; it warns us against assuming that reality is simply what we can see – or understand. To speak of God as a 'mystery' is to acknowledge that we have been grasped by something and someone greater than ourselves, compelling us to stretch, rather than limit, the horizons of our awareness.

So how can we make sure that we have appreciated the fullness of the Christian faith? That we have done justice to the richness and wonder of God? That we have comprehended the full significance of Jesus Christ? There is a way of thinking about this that is especially helpful, and we shall consider it in the next section.

Rainbows and brushstrokes

It was a brilliant Tuscan morning back in 1988. I had travelled to Florence to work on some unpublished fifteenth-century manuscripts that were held by one of the great Renaissance libraries in the city. The library was set around a small courtyard, like a monastic cloister, and had stone walkways, roofed with the brilliant red tiles for which Florence is famous, arranged around its four sides. At the centre of the courtyard was a small garden. Plants grew in profusion within the garden, as they did over the masonry of the building itself.

With all the enthusiasm of a scholar working abroad, I had turned up far too early. The library was closed. As I waited for it to open, I walked around the courtyard and noticed that the garden took on completely different aspects depending on where I stood. From one angle, it seemed to be dominated by roses; from another, by citrus trees. To fully appreciate it, I had to see it from every side. Each of the great arched glassless windows in the courtyard opened up to give a different view of the same garden. Each view was like a snapshot, building up to give a composite picture of a greater whole.

The librarian arrived. I gathered my papers together and prepared to start work for the day. My sense of anticipation was, however, rapidly flattened. She explained to me that as it was a Monday, the library opened even later than usual. Dejected, I wandered off to a nearby square and ordered a cup of coffee at one of its many pavement cafés. I tried to console myself by reflecting that the manuscripts had been in the library for 500 years and would probably survive another hour or two.

The square was next to the Duomo, Florence's great Renaissance cathedral. From my seat I had a marvellous view of a small section of it, and after finishing my coffee and consulting my watch, I decided to spend the remainder of my time exploring its magnificent interior. I pottered around pretending I was Lucy Honeychurch in E. M. Forster's classic novel *A Room with a View*. Finally, I returned to the now open library and immersed myself in my studies.

But the events of that morning remained in my mind. I reflected that the bigger and more complicated something is, the more difficult it is to take in at a single glance. The garden illustrated this point neatly, the cathedral more graphically. It is no good glancing over at a wonderful building from the window of a passing coach or a seat at a pavement café. You have to get out and explore it from all kinds of angles and viewpoints, otherwise its riches and wonders will remain largely hidden and undiscovered. It may have been 'seen' – but it has not been understood or appreciated. Snapshots of the different aspects of a great building help us piece together the panoramic vision that each, by itself, fails to disclose. To put it simply: the whole turns out to be greater than the sum of its parts. Yet each part matters.

My difficulty in getting a full view of even a little garden helped me to appreciate the problems we face trying to take in the glorious riches of the Christian faith. There is just too much to squeeze into a neat little formula, a single sentence or a simple analogy. The great matters of faith – such as the nature of God or the identity of Jesus Christ – are complex.

For example, the Bible uses a wide range of similes and analogies to help us grasp the significance of God. To mention only a few: God is our Father; God is our shepherd; God is a rock. And so on. The same is true of Jesus of Nazareth. He is the Messiah, the Son of David, the saviour, and the friend of sinners. Again, when we come to think about the meaning of the cross, we find the Bible and the long Christian tradition of reflection on the biblical texts saturated with images and ideas, illuminating its significance. The cross reveals the love of God. It enables the forgiveness of sins. It brings healing. In every case, a rich and multi-faceted reality is represented by a series of snapshots. Our task is to piece together the panorama that each of these snapshots individually discloses in part. Seeing the 'big picture' expands our vision of faith; reflecting on its individual elements allows us to deepen our understanding. Two analogies will make this point clearer.

Imagine a rainbow. The raindrops cause the white light of the sun to break down into its individual components – red, orange, yellow, green, blue, indigo and violet. The colours are all there, combined in white light. But the process of refraction, which takes place within the raindrops, allows each of those components to be seen and appreciated individually.

Or consider a striking painting – such as Van Gogh's famous sunflowers. We stand back and take in the whole picture, appreciating it as a work of art. Then we move closer, admiring Van Gogh's individual brushstrokes and his brilliant use of colour and texture.

To appreciate our faith to the full, we need to grasp the big picture and explore the fine detail. We need to see the panorama and examine the individual snapshots. The French intellectual historian Etienne Gilson (1884–1978) once suggested that medieval theology was like a 'cathedral of the mind'. This fits well with our recent contemplation of

Florence's Duomo. Imagine inhabiting this vast, magnificent cathedral, and the excitement of exploring its many aspects – its design, its beauty, its splendour.

To return to the creeds, we may say that far from merely summing up the things of God, they are an invitation to explore the wonders to which they point. Like diagrams of cathedrals and maps of landscapes, they are useful as summaries and starting points, but come to life when we let them guide us on a voyage of discovery, in which we see things with new eyes and take things in with a new sense of satisfaction.

Let's now explore how the creeds actually came into being.

4

The creeds: a public vision of faith

One of my most vivid childhood memories involves going to church in rural Ireland back in the 1950s. The congregation was asked to recite the Athanasian Creed, using the language of the old Prayer Book. We got to the complicated bit about 'the Father incomprehensible, the Son incomprehensible, and the Holy Ghost incomprehensible'. An old farmer then interrupted proceedings by declaring that 'the whole darned thing's incomprehensible'. And he had my sympathy. The words meant nothing to me, and may even have helped me lurch into my atheist phase a few years later.

Many Christians will know exactly what that old farmer meant. The creeds often seem wordy and formulaic. Yet they are verbal vessels containing the treasure of the gospel. We need to regard them as a window to look through, or a lens to bring things into focus. They are not an end in themselves, but a means to an end – and that end is catching sight of the life-changing vision of God.

Creeds and the life of faith

We often think of faith as checklists of beliefs. You begin by deciding whether you believe in God. Having sorted that out, you then move on to the next item on the list. And when

you finally get to the end, you can say, 'Amen! Yes, I believe!'
But faith's not really like that. It's much more about catching
a vision of the big picture that lies at the heart of Christianity,
being drawn to it and beginning to explore it further. Or like
falling in love with someone and then wanting to know more
about them. Loving and trusting come first. Finding out
more comes later.

Consider the Gospel accounts of the calling of Peter and
Andrew, the fishermen Jesus of Nazareth encountered on the
shores of Lake Galilee (Mark 1.16–20). Jesus speaks these
simple words to them: 'Come, follow me.' No explanation
is offered of who he is. But finding Jesus to be an utterly
compelling figure, the first disciples leave behind their
nets – on which their living depended completely – and
follow. They choose to entrust themselves totally to him,
discerning that he is someone truly special yet not quite
understanding who.

We might think wistfully that it is a pity things could not
have stayed so simple. The first disciples were not required
to recite a creed before they were allowed to follow Jesus!
So why do we need them today? If the heart of faith is about
entrusting ourselves to Jesus Christ, why make it more
complicated?

These are perfectly fair questions. Perhaps we need to
remember, however, that although Peter's and Andrew's
journey of faith began on the shores of Lake Galilee, it did
not end there. As we read the Gospels, we recognize that the
disciples' faith deepens as they gradually come to understand
more about the identity and significance of Jesus of Nazareth.
In the beginning, they trust him; as time passes, this personal
trust is supplemented with – but never displaced by – beliefs
about him as they work through a series of questions. How

does Jesus of Nazareth fit into the story of Israel? What is so special about this person? What are the implications of following him? How will he impact their own personal stories? It is in answering these questions and explaining to others why Jesus was so important that the disciples find themselves having to use *words* to express their *beliefs* about him. The creeds are the carefully chosen words that the early Church agreed on to try and capture what lay at the heart of the Christian faith. They describe the Christian faith as a sketch map describes a landscape.

Another way we might think of the creeds is as a skeleton that supports the life-giving organs of faith. Without its rigid framework, the human body would collapse, unable to support itself. Its network of interconnected bones provides stability and structure to the organs that are necessary for life – the heart, pumping blood around the body; the lungs, transferring life-giving oxygen to the bloodstream; and the arteries and veins, transporting the blood to the sites at which it is needed. These organs really matter. But they need the skeleton for support if they are to work properly.

Taken on their own, away from the context of a living faith, the creeds are simply a collection of words. They can be recited by people who have no idea of their potential significance. Think of a medical student's skeleton: it is a symbol of death because the vital organs that give life to the body are not there. A creed could be a statement of a faith that has gone cold and become quite lifeless – something that is merely *recited*, when it is meant to be *trusted*.

Yet the creeds are not meant to be taken on their own, in isolation. They are part of a greater whole – the external protective shell of the inner living reality of faith based on a loving relationship with God, through Jesus Christ, in the power of the Holy Spirit. And the vital organs of such a faith are prayer, worship and adoration.

Faith, belief and creeds

The two main creeds of the Christian churches (the Apostles' Creed and the Nicene Creed; see the Appendix) are familiar to many, mainly because they are so widely used in Christian worship. But why are they there? Do we really need them? After all, no other major world religion uses creeds – not even other monotheistic faiths, such as Judaism or Islam, which clearly have quite definite beliefs. Let's begin exploring these questions by looking at faith at its simplest – as an act of trust – and see where this takes us.

One of the most moving scenes in the Gospels concerns the two criminals who were crucified with Jesus Christ at Calvary. The first, representing a world-weary cynicism, ridicules Christ. The second, however, recognizes that there is something different about him. Though unsure how to put this insight into words, he knows that this man is to be depended upon. 'Jesus, remember me when you come into your kingdom' (Luke 23.43). His simple statement of confidence and entrustment lacks theological rigour, but it is enough. Christ's response has resonated down the ages: 'Truly I tell you, today you will be with me in Paradise.'

The crucified criminal – about whom we know nothing, not even his name – is a model of Christian faith. He demonstrates what really matters: a deep and passionate conviction that he can hand himself over to Jesus. He trusts him. Many of us are drawn to Christ in his strange loneliness on the cross and intuitively realize that he holds the key to life. Theological refinement can easily come after personal commitment has taken place.

With this point in mind, Christian writers down the ages have distinguished two senses of the word 'faith'. First, it refers to a 'faith by which we believe' – that is to say, the act of trust and assent that says 'yes' to God and reaches out to hold fast to God as the secure ground of life and thought. Second, it refers to a 'faith which we believe' – that is to say, a set of beliefs. In this sense of the word, faith refers to the content of what we believe rather than the act of believing and trusting. Although these two ways of understanding the word 'faith' are inseparable in that they are like two sides of the same coin, it is nevertheless helpful to distinguish between them. Creeds relate mainly to faith in the second sense of the word – but they presuppose faith in the first sense.

Having faith in God is about trusting God. Beliefs represent an attempt to put the substance of that faith into words. While creeds are secondary to our trust and commitment, that does not mean that they are unimportant or that we can do without them. The relationship between the believer and God, expressed in prayer and worship, needs to be explored in words and ideas. The medieval theologian Anselm of Canterbury (*c.*1033–1109) made this point in his slogan 'faith seeking understanding'. We are called upon to love God with our minds, as well as our hearts and souls (Matthew 22.37). Part of the life of faith is a desire to understand more about who and what we trust.

G. K. Chesterton had much to say on this, suggesting that a human being was 'an animal that makes dogmas'. Trees, he observed, 'have no dogmas'. Everyone is an agnostic until agnosticism fails them in moments of crisis and need. The person who boldly proclaims that 'humanity needs freedom from dogma' is, Chesterton suggests, like a scientist confidently asserting that 'people can live without oxygen'. Creeds, whether explicit or implicit, religious or secular, are just part of human existence.

Dorothy L. Sayers made a similar point. She ridiculed those who, in the name of 'tolerance', refused to believe anything. This cynical disengagement from the big questions of life, she wrote, 'believes in nothing, cares for nothing, seeks to know nothing, interferes with nothing, enjoys nothing, hates nothing, finds purpose in nothing, lives for nothing, and remains alive because there is nothing for which it will die'. This, she declared, was not an affirmation of tolerance; it was a confession of despair.

Sayers is correct. We just can't live without structures of meaning. And when you find the answers to these questions, you hang on to them. Why? Because they matter. They make a difference. Cynics believe that there are no answers to the big questions of life, and get angry with those who have found them, secretly fearing that those answers might be right. The person who defiantly asserts 'I have no creed' very often really means, 'I don't want to think about deep questions, as I am worried that I might find answers that turn out to be inconvenient.'

That was what C. S. Lewis discovered as he pondered life's big questions back in the 1920s. He didn't want to believe in God. He found the idea threatening, not least because it would compromise his independence. 'Amiable agnostics will talk cheerfully about "man's search for God". To me, as I then was, they might as well have talked about the mouse's search for the cat.'[1] Yet he gradually realized that he had no options. God was not just an idea, but a living reality who was drawing near to Lewis personally. What he had once thought of as a 'philosophical theorem, cerebrally entertained, began to stir and heave and throw off its graveclothes, and stood upright and became a living presence'.[2] He found that he could resist God no longer. So he stepped into a new world, as 'the most reluctant convert in all England', and began to explore its landscape.

Christian creeds set out a framework of meaning that we can use to position ourselves on the map of history and make sense of things around us. In what follows, we will explore how the creeds emerged, what role they played and how they help shape Christian thought and life today.

How the creeds emerged

For the first three centuries, Christians managed to get along without any formal creeds. This was not because they had no interest in what they believed, but simply because there were no agreed universal public norms of faith throughout the Christian world. It's not hard to see what the problem was. At its height, in the early second century, the Roman Empire included the entire Mediterranean region. Christianity spread through this area with astonishing speed, but because it was an illegal religion, its believers were forced to meet in secret to worship. There was no way Christian leaders could gather together to discuss a common set of beliefs: the risk of arrest by the Roman authorities was simply too great.

Yet the historical records show a remarkable degree of consensus emerging within the Christian world of the late second century. For reasons that are not fully understood, believers throughout the Roman Empire were beginning to converge on a particular set of writings that they read aloud in public worship and regarded as authoritative in matters of life and thought. There were local variations of course, but by around 190 we can begin to see collections of texts very similar to the modern New Testament taking shape, along with 'confessions of faith' that looked a lot like the modern Apostles' Creed.

These collections of texts and confessions of faith were used by individual congregations, and seem to have been adopted primarily through the movement of Christians across imperial frontiers. Certain congregations were particularly highly regarded and tended to set the trend for others. The leaders of Christian communities in the metropolitan cities – such as Alexandria, Antioch, Jerusalem and Rome – developed their own distinct ways of teaching the faith, giving rise to prototypes of the creeds. Those used in Rome were especially significant, on account of the status of Rome as the 'eternal city', the capital of the empire.

Admission to Christian worship was a serious and solemn matter. New Christians only gained entry once they had been carefully vetted (they might, after all, be Roman spies) and thoroughly instructed in the basics. At baptism, which marked formal admission to the Christian community, believers were asked to confirm their faith, by responding to three questions:

1 Do you believe in God the Father Almighty?
2 Do you believe in Jesus Christ, the Son of God?
3 Do you believe in the Holy Spirit?

Though these questions were sometimes asked in more extended and elaborate forms, this basic threefold pattern was widely used in both the western and eastern churches. In part, it reflects the 'Great Commission' of the risen Christ to his disciples: 'Go therefore and make disciples of all nations, baptizing them in the name of the Father and of the Son and of the Holy Spirit' (Matthew 28.19). By answering 'I believe' to each question, the person who was about to be baptized was affirming his commitment to the Christian way of thinking – to its overall big picture, not simply to three of its components.

The 'rules of faith'

From the end of the second century, documents that are clearly recognizable as creeds began to be used by prominent churches and Christian leaders as convenient summaries of faith. Although slightly different forms of words appeared across the Christian world, the shared features of these statements are more obvious than their minor divergences. The statements gradually became known as *regulae fidei* (a Latin phrase meaning 'rules of faith'). Tertullian (*c*.160–*c*.225), a Latin-speaking theologian writing in the early third century, provided one of his own. Christians, he declared, believed:

> . . . that there is one only God, the Creator of the world, who produced all things out of nothing through his own Word, sent forth first of all; that this Word is called his Son, and, under the name of God, was seen in various ways by the patriarchs, heard at all times in the prophets, at last brought down by the Spirit and Power of the Father into the Virgin Mary, was made flesh in her womb, and, being born of her, went forth as Jesus Christ; he then preached the new law and the new promise of the kingdom of heaven, and worked miracles; having been crucified, he rose again on the third day; having ascended into the heavens, he sat at the right hand of the Father; sent in his place the power of the Holy Spirit to guide those who believe; and will come with glory to take the saints to the enjoyment of everlasting life and of the heavenly promises.[3]

Despite some obvious differences, there are remarkable simi-larities between Tertullian's 'rule of faith' and the Apostles' Creed. Both these and other rules of faith commanded respect on account of their merits, and were adopted and adapted over a period of several generations, until a degree of consensus emerged. The Apostles' Creed was the final outcome of a long process of reflection and refinement across the Christian world, leading to a rule of faith that was accepted not on account of any external authority, but because of its internal excellence.

The Apostles' Creed served two important functions. First, it was a shared statement of faith, easily memorized through constant repetition in public worship, through which new Christians could confess and summarize their faith in Jesus Christ. And second, it served as a highly useful preaching and teaching tool, giving an outline of the basic themes of faith for further discussion and exploration, especially in sermons.

So what of the Nicene Creed? To understand the develop-ment of this document, we need to appreciate the radical change to the status of Christianity in the early fourth cen-tury, as a result of the conversion of the Roman emperor Constantine. Christianity was now a legal religion. Its laity and leaders were no longer subject to any form of state harassment, victimization or persecution. Christian worship no longer had to take place in secret. Christian leaders were free to meet and travel.

As Christianity moved towards becoming the state religion of the Roman Empire, the Roman emperor Constantine made it clear that he expected it to fulfil the functions of classical Roman religion – above all, by acting as a unifying force. Divisions within Christianity had to be sorted out, so that the Church could both model and encourage the unity that Constantine wished to see prevail throughout his empire.

There were several issues of contention within Christianity at this time, including the status of the bishops of the leading cities of the age. Christianity had firmly established itself in the great cities of Rome, Alexandria and Antioch. It also had an important presence in the ancient city of Jerusalem. So which church took priority within the empire? Who was the most senior bishop? (In the end, Rome was given pride of place.) Other divisions of a more theological nature included, most notably, the best way of expressing the identity and significance of Jesus Christ.

Constantine summoned a council of Christian bishops. They met in 325 at the town of Nicaea in Asia Minor (modern-day Turkey), and the agreement they reached on these matters formed the basis of a new creed. (What we now know as the 'Nicene Creed' is actually a later version of the creed of 325, agreed at the Council of Chalcedon in 451.) This 325 creed was imposed on the Church by its bishops and the emperor. Notably, it did not initially command the strong popular consensus that the Apostles' Creed had won over many generations.

So we see – although the point is not generally appreciated – that the two most widely used creeds within Christianity today developed in quite different ways. The Apostles' Creed arose within grass-root Christian communities over many generations, and commanded wide assent and support. The Nicene Creed was developed by a committee of bishops, in response to the Roman emperor's demand for religious consensus within his empire. There has always been a sense in which the Apostles' Creed is a 'people's creed', whereas the Nicene Creed is a 'bishops' creed'.

This brief historical account of the origins of the two main creeds in widespread use today helps us understand how they came about. But it does not offer an explanation for their statements. We need to dig deeper if we are to make sense of the specific form they take.

Weaving together biblical themes

A central function of Christian creeds is that they weave together the great themes found in the Bible. Early Christian statements of faith were often very short – for example, the simple confession, 'Jesus is Lord!' (Romans 10.9; 1 Corinthians 12.3). Yet the New Testament also contains a number of slightly longer creed-like statements, such as the following:

> There is one God, the Father, from whom are all things and for whom we exist, and one Lord, Jesus Christ, through whom are all things and through whom we exist.   (1 Corinthians 8.6)

> I handed on to you as of first importance what I in turn had received: that Christ died for our sins in accordance with the scriptures, and that he was buried, and that he was raised on the third day in accordance with the scriptures.
> (1 Corinthians 15.3–4)

> [Jesus Christ] was revealed in flesh, vindicated in spirit, seen by angels, proclaimed among Gentiles, believed in throughout the world, taken up in glory.   (1 Timothy 3.16)

These and other similar statements are scattered throughout the biblical texts. They are not integrated into what we might today call a 'systematic theology'. The New Testament letters, for example, bring together wise advice on living in a non-Christian world, reflections on how Christian families should behave, instructions on conducting public worship, and invaluable nuggets of theological teaching.

But what of those who want more information specifically about Christian beliefs? Christian writers have always been clear that the creeds do not add anything to the Bible. Their function is to summarize its leading themes and provide a framework for understanding its overall concerns. Cyril of Jerusalem (*c.*313–86) made this point well in the fourth century. After asking his readers to commit the creed to memory and engrave it on their hearts, he explained its relation to the Bible.

> This synthesis of faith was made . . . to present the one teaching of the faith in its totality, in which what is of greatest importance is gathered together from all the Scriptures. And just as a mustard seed contains a great number of branches in its tiny grain, so also this summary of faith brings together in a few words the entire knowledge of the true religion which is contained in the Old and New Testaments.[4]

Cyril's approach – which clearly draws on that of earlier writers – has found widespread acceptance within all the Christian churches. The creed is not a personal statement of faith, drawn up by an individual (however important); it is a public statement of the faith of the Christian community, which developed within those communities as they reflected on their rich heritage and sought to express this as succinctly as possible.

Yet it is clear that there are biblical topics many would regard as important that are not discussed in either of the creeds. For example, there is no reference to the relation of the Christian Church and Israel, or to Jesus Christ representing the fulfilment of Old Testament prophecy – a major theme in Matthew's Gospel and some of Paul's letters. The Apostles' Creed leaves out any explicit reference to the divinity of Christ, a major theme of the Nicene Creed.

But if the creeds do not – and were never intended to – displace the Bible, they certainly offer a framework for interpreting it. This is one of the major themes in Christian theology – how to achieve the 'right' or 'best' interpretation of the Bible – and has always been important, even in early Christianity. Irenaeus of Lyons, a key theologian of the second century, complained that some mavericks were interpreting the Bible in ways that bore no relation to Christianity, and argued that they had no right to do this. He believed that the way in which the apostles read the Bible was normative for Christians. What the New Testament calls the 'deposit of faith' (1 Timothy 6.19) refers to the fundamental themes of the Christian faith, entrusted to the apostles and passed on to their successors. In effect, Irenaeus argued that we inherited two things from the apostles: the texts that we now call the New Testament, and the right way of interpreting these texts. Irenaeus saw the 'apostolic tradition' as a safeguard against misunderstanding and misrepresentation of the Bible.

The creeds sum up the Christian community's extended reflections on how best to make sense of the Bible and weave its threads together to give the most satisfactory and authentic account of faith. They are keys to unlocking the Bible – a map to enable us to find treasure rather than the treasure itself.

Let's linger here for a moment. In the great age of exploration, European seafarers opened up new trade routes from Europe to Asia, including the newly discovered Americas. They kept a record of their voyages, telling of the landmarks by which they set their course, safe harbours in which to shelter from storms, and dangerous reefs that might sink a ship. These journals were called 'rutters' (from the French word *routier*, 'a map'). They were a summary of a navigator's experience, which could be passed down to others to allow them to make the same journey.

The creeds are a rutter of faith. They tell how the Christian community of faith navigated its way to the best interpretation of the Bible, and pass down to us their experiences, in order that we might benefit from them. Our forebears wrestled with these questions before us, and we can learn from their wisdom. At times the creeds tell of reefs that are to be avoided – such as Jesus of Nazareth simply being 'like' God. At times they tell us about safe anchorages – such as the doctrine of the Trinity, which the early Christians found to be a reliable and rich summary of the biblical witness.

This brings us to a theme that is clearly hinted at by the creeds – the importance of connecting with the Christian past.

Solidarity with the Christian past

As we have seen, early versions of the Apostles' Creed began to emerge in Christian communities spread across the Roman Empire in the second and third centuries. The confession of Christian faith was regarded by the authorities as subversive, and those who admitted to being Christians in Rome were liable to be executed.

Justin Martyr (100–165), a Christian theologian based in the city, was arrested in 165. At his trial before the Roman prefect, he refused to worship or sacrifice to the traditional

Roman gods, and instead declared his faith in the following terms:

> We worship the God of the Christians, whom we believe to be one from the beginning, the maker and fashioner of the whole creation, visible and invisible; and the Lord Jesus Christ, the Son of God, whose coming to be present with the human race as the herald of salvation and teacher of good disciples had been proclaimed beforehand by the prophets.[5]

It is a recognizable precedent of modern creeds; and uttering it cost Justin his life. He was beheaded as a martyr.

We are beginning to see that reciting the Apostles' Creed involves rather more than simply checklisting our convictions. For in reconnecting us with Christian family history – as we honour and celebrate the faith and witness of earlier generations of believers whose confession led them into danger and death – the creed assumes a new significance. We might regard it as a roll-call of Christian witnesses down the ages, a precious heirloom, like the family silver, passed down from one generation to another.

This great theme of acting in solidarity with the saints, martyrs and ordinary believers of the past is set out in the 'bidding prayer' of the Service of Nine Lessons and Carols at King's College, Cambridge (in a different section from the one we looked at in Chapter 3):

> Let us remember before God all those who rejoice with us, but upon another shore, and in a greater light, that multitude which no man can number, whose hope was in the Word made flesh, and with whom in the Lord Jesus we are for ever one.

Knowing that reciting the creeds aligns us with a community of faithful believers stretching back into the days of the Roman Empire is both exciting and humbling. It invites us to recognize that a 'great cloud of witnesses' (Hebrews 12.1) surrounds us as we ourselves run the race of faith in the amphitheatre of the world. Those who have already completed that race are cheering us on, as we struggle to keep going.

If the words of the creeds have become dulled by familiarity, remember that our forebears in Christ are encouraging us to view them afresh as an act of defiance and self-definition, as a refusal to compromise and a mark of discipleship. When you say the creed, see yourself as in the presence of the martyrs and saints of old, who used these same words to confess that same faith and who smile on us as we try to live out our faith in the world.

There is another point worth considering here. Those who made the journey of faith before us can help us as we undertake the same pilgrimage. They asked the same questions we ask, and their answers can encourage us as we wrestle today. The great medieval theologian John of Salisbury (1120–80) used a memorable image to help us think about this point.

> We are sitting on the shoulders of giants. We see more, and things that are more distant, than they did, not because our sight is superior or because we are taller than they were, but because they raise us up, and by their great stature add to ours.[6]

C. S. Lewis often pointed out that we need an enlargement of our vision of divine reality. The great writings of Christians down the ages enable us 'to see with other eyes, to imagine with other imaginations, to feel with other hearts, as well as our own'.[7] We read Christian classics to expand our vision of our faith, by allowing these writers to help us go further and deeper into our faith. This is not a dead traditionalism that values the past simply because of its age; it is a living faith that values the wisdom of the past because it remains so valuable and useful. The famous American church historian Jaroslav Pelikan (1923–2006) put this nicely: 'Tradition is the living faith of the dead; traditionalism is the dead faith of the living.'

The creeds are a reminder of the importance of intergenerational transmission of faith, in which one generation hands down to the next the words, ideas, practices and images that it has found helpful in expressing and nourishing its faith. C. S. Lewis observed that we live in an age of 'chronological snobbery' that believes that the most recent is the best. For Lewis, older approaches often represent tried and tested ways that have proved to be reliable and trustworthy down the ages. We need to keep 'the clean sea breeze of the centuries blowing through our minds',[8] to clear away the fog and enable us to think clearly. Others have pondered the great questions of life and faith before us. Why should we not benefit from their wisdom?

Growing into the creeds

The creeds are primarily communal confessions of faith, setting out the vision of reality that has given – and still gives – life, purpose and direction to the Christian community down the ages. When I recite the creeds, I think of myself as doing three things. First, I am remembering the 'big picture' that underlies the Christian faith. Second, I am affirming that I am part of this believing community. And third, I am declaring my willingness to explore what I have not yet encountered and affirm what I have not yet understood.

The creeds are aspirational: they set out a vision that they invite us to share, even though many of us are still exploring individual aspects of that vision.

At this point some will possibly want to raise a concern, such as: 'Yes, I do indeed believe and trust in God. But the creeds say some things that I can't quite understand. And there are some bits that I'm not sure about at all!'

However, let's remember that Christianity is about a big picture. Part of the life of faith is growing into it. Things that don't make much sense to begin with can grow clearer later. When I first became a Christian, I found the idea of the Trinity to be very strange and puzzling. Now, I can see what it's all about. We simply have to take some things on trust and never limit the Christian vision of reality to that which we have personally experienced, understood or grasped. Others, past and present, urge us to go further and deeper. For example, when Paul speaks of the 'boundless' or 'unsearchable' riches of Christ (Ephesians 3.8), he is not *prohibiting* us from investigating further, but *encouraging* us to do so. We are to be caught up in the proper and enriching exploration of something that is greater and more wonderful than we realize.

Reciting the creeds is thus about both affirming what we have already discovered and come to trust, and setting an agenda for the enlargement of our appreciation of God and Christ.

Creeds and Christian identity

One of the many challenges faced by early Christians was that of intellectual or religious assimilation. Christians were clear that their faith set them apart from the world-views around them, whether these were religious or secular. Christian believers and communities were called to be the 'salt of the earth'. But what if the salt were to lose its saltiness?

As Christianity became a growing presence within the Roman Empire, it faced pressure to conform to Roman religious and cultural norms and drop its distinctive identity. Hippolytus of Rome (*c.*170–*c.*236) compared the Church to a boat, tossed about in a stormy ocean. 'The world is a sea in which the Church, like a ship, is beaten by the waves, but not submerged.' Yet the risk of being swamped by the prevailing culture was real. The integrity of the Church had to be preserved if it was to survive.

The creeds were a way in which Christian identity could be affirmed, maintained and safeguarded. Reciting the creed was a way of ensuring that individual believers and their communities were *different*. The creeds reminded believers of their real identity and goal. Although their physical bodies might be rooted in the world in which they lived and worked, the big picture of reality set out by the creeds meant that their hopes lay elsewhere. A Christian might be a Roman citizen, but this was far less important than also being a citizen of heaven.

This issue remains important today, especially where Christianity has been of major historical significance. In the United States of America, Christianity can too easily become part of a general cultural package, a kind of 'civil religion' that provides a religious veneer for American culture. However, Christianity is not, and must not be allowed to be, simply a bastion of traditional values. For example, although some argue that the churches ought to be defenders of trad- itional notions of marriage, we find nothing of this idea in the New Testament or early Christianity. It is dangerous to think of churches simply as repositories of the past, lending religious weight to cultural values that are seen to be under threat.

This point was famously made in a lecture entitled 'Creed or Chaos?' given in England during the Second World War by Dorothy L. Sayers. Many were worried about the threat to traditional moral values posed by the rise of Nazism, and the rapid military advance of German armies across Western Europe. Sayers argued that moral values reflect a dogma on which they depended for their credibility. British intellectuals, anxious to get rid of Christian ideas but keep its moral framework, had failed to realize that you cannot sustain Christian values without the world-view on which they are based. Nazi beliefs gave rise to one set of moral values; Christian beliefs to another. You can't keep Christian ethics without also keeping the Christian world-view. Sayers ridiculed secularists who were trying 'to uphold a particular standard of ethical values which derives from Christian dogma' while at the same time trying to get rid of 'the very dogma which is the sole rational foundation for those values'.[9]

In the end, Sayers declared, this real battle was not about moral values, but about the world-views on which these values were based. Safeguarding Christian distinctiveness is the essential precondition for safeguarding Christian values. The creeds set out Christianity's distinct 'take' on reality and reminded Christians that, in the end, their life and thought are shaped by this view. Without a creed there would be moral chaos. A 'doctrineless' Christianity is simply an impossibility, in that Christians think – and need to think and must be encouraged to think – about the nature of their faith and its implications for the way they live.

We have spent quite some time exploring the nature of Christian belief and the place of creeds in the Christian life. Yet we still need to reflect a little more on one of the great themes of Christianity – the difference that beliefs make to the way we live. This we shall do in the next chapter, as we consider the opening statement of the creeds: 'I believe'.

5

'I believe': stepping into the 'big picture'

'I believe'. To some, these opening words of the creeds sound flat and weak. Yet there is a hidden strength in them, for these words declare that we have found an answer to life's deepest questions. We have discovered a place of refuge, a safe anchorage for the soul and a firm place on which to stand. Martin Luther (1486–1543) pointed out that everyone needs to base their lives on something or someone. 'Your god is whatever you have set your heart upon, the one in whom you trust.'[1]

Luther suggested that faith is like a boat that you believe can take you from an island to the shore, even in rough seas. But do you have sufficient confidence to get in and set sail? Faith is about both trust and entrustment.

Knowing whom and what we can rely on is of enormous importance. Back in the days when I was a science research student a fellow student needed to get to Heathrow airport to catch an early morning flight for a job interview in Zurich. I asked him how he planned to make sure he was there in time. He smiled. He would be driven by a close friend who had promised to pick him up at four o'clock the following morning for the hour-long drive. I was surprised at this, as the person concerned had a well-earned reputation for being totally unreliable. But maybe, I thought to myself, I had misjudged things.

I met my friend a few days later and asked him how the interview went. He was crestfallen. He had never made it to Zurich. In fact, he had never even made it to the airport. The person who had promised to drive him there had completely forgotten and failed to turn up. (The interview was later rearranged, but my friend didn't get the job.)

We learn, often the hard way, that some people are trustworthy and reliable and others are not. Time and time again, we read of people entrusting their life savings to 'experts' who promise to make them rich quickly. A month later, their savings – and the 'experts' – have disappeared. You may feel that it is a good and Christian thing to place confidence in others – but that doesn't necessarily mean that they are going to prove worthy of our trust.

Faith, trust and security

The creeds tell us whom we may trust and where we may find security. More than that, they reassure us that countless people in the past have found them a tried and tested way of summing up the essentials of faith. Others have unlocked the door of the mystery of life and handed down to us the keys, so that we might use them.

The opening words of the creeds – 'I believe' – suggest that the focus of faith is the individual. Now there is much to be said for such a way of looking at things. One great theme of classical understandings of the Christian faith is that it transforms personal existence. The Gospel accounts of the ministry of Jesus Christ, for example, often speak of individuals (such as Zacchaeus: Luke 19.1–10) whose lives are changed through an encounter with him.

The Christian 'big picture' insists that each individual believer is significant. We are known to God by name and will retain our personal identity in the New Jerusalem. There is no question of being swallowed up, like a drop of water in a vast ocean, losing whatever it is that makes us distinctive. The statement 'I have faith in God' finds its echo in our realization that God knows and loves each one of us.

Yet Christianity is a corporate faith. As countless Christian writers have discovered down the ages, the life of faith is at its most authentic when we relate to other believers. We help one another to go deeper into the riches of our shared faith; we support one another in our trials; we affirm one another's strengths, and we work to deal with one another's weaknesses. Dietrich Bonhoeffer's famous work *Life Together* (1938), is one of many to emphasize that the Christian community arises naturally from the core themes of the Christian faith.

> Because God has already laid the only foundation of our fellowship, because God has bound us together in one body with other Christians in Jesus Christ, long before we entered into common life with them, we enter into that common life not as demanders but as thankful recipients.[2]

For this reason, reciting the creeds is to be seen as an act of corporate witness, not simply a personal confession of faith. It is not I alone who has put my trust in God; it is the community of faith down the ages that shares this faith with me. In using the creed to frame my faith, I am aligning myself with this community and affirming that I belong to it. We see the world of experience in the light of a world of beliefs.

The creeds thus help prevent us from lapsing into a maverick individualism ('This is the way I see it – so it must be right') or an impoverished account of faith that misses out on the riches that other Christians have discovered before us and around us. Christianity needs to be constantly refreshed by living springs of water. The creeds are like channels, connecting us with both the fountainhead of faith and the faithful reflections of those who have inhabited its landscape in the past.

The opening words of the creed are as much an invitation as they are an affirmation. They invite us to share the faith of Abraham, who trusted God's promises and set out into the unknown (Genesis 12.1–4), and the myriads who came after him, whose trust was in this same joy-giving, life-changing God. Yes, Christianity is about certain ideas that we believe; but it is more fundamentally about a God whom we discover to be trustworthy and allow to become the foundation and lodestar of our lives.

Christianity allows us to see things as they really are, and points us to something (and someone) we can trust. Faith is about finding security in life, being anchored to God, who is our 'rock of refuge' and our 'strong fortress' (Psalm 31.2). Looking out from this place of safety, we can see the landscape of the world as it really is, illuminated by God. Perhaps this is what the Psalmist has in mind when he declared (Psalm 27.1):

> The LORD is my light and my salvation; whom shall I fear?
> The LORD is the stronghold of my life; of whom shall I be afraid?

Faith is 'the assurance of things hoped for, the conviction of things not seen' (Hebrews 11.1). We walk in faith and hope, not in full possession of all we will one day inherit, but with one foot in that new and coming kingdom. Though based in this world, we are anchored in the next. Faith is about reaching out towards things to come, embracing and anticipating that future joy. It is about trusting the big picture of the Christian faith and stepping into it, knowing that we are meant to be part of this picture and not merely external observers. This point is so important that we need to explore it further.

Stepping into the 'big picture'

There are three basic questions we need to ask about any Christian belief. First, why do we think this is true? What reasons can we give for believing it? Second, how can we make sense of this? What is the best way of explaining it? And third, what difference does a belief make? If it is right, how does it affect the way we live?

In this final chapter of this introductory volume we will focus on this third question as we prepare for a lively and stimulating exploration of Christian beliefs in the four volumes to follow. If a given Christian belief – such as the doctrine of the incarnation or Trinity – is true, how does it change the way in which we think and live? To answer this important question, let's think more about the Christian big picture – the rich and capacious way of seeing things that is hard-wired into the Christian faith.

Earlier (p. 29), we noted Evelyn Waugh's description of how his new Christian faith allowed him to see things clearly for the first time. Let's look very closely at the way he phrased this discovery, reading his words slowly to make sure that we appreciate the power of the image he uses.

> Conversion is like stepping across the chimney piece out of a Looking-Glass world, where everything is an absurd carica-ture, into the real world God made; and then begins the delicious process of exploring it limitlessly.

What Waugh is describing is leaving behind a distorted and illusory world, entering into the real world God made – what we know as the big picture of the Christian faith – and dis-covering the difference this makes to his thought and life.

I remember watching the film *Mary Poppins* when it first came out in 1964. It was a wonderful movie, telling the story of how the arrival of a new nanny sprinkled stardust on the dull and respectable life of a banker's family in Edwardian London. One scene entranced me. Julie Andrews and Dick Van Dyke stop to admire a chalk drawing on a London street – and then step into it, thus entering a new world. Part of me dismissed this as sentimental nonsense. But another part of me delighted in this imaginative adventure. The won-der of stepping into another world!

We've already seen how the Christian faith invites us not simply to look *at* Christian beliefs, but to look *through* them, and thus enter a world in which we view things in new ways. We no longer simply 'see' the big picture; we step inside it and become part of it. By faith, we are citizens of a new and better country, with the right to inhabit it – and the desire to explore it. The creeds offer us a map of this new world, a lens through which we can bring its landscapes into focus and a light that illuminates its shadowlands. The creeds are there to help us explore this world, find our way around it and above all get used to living within it.

Thinking about this world

Now that we realize this world is a land through which we pass on our way to our true home, rather than being our true home itself, we can look at it in new ways, and no longer need to regard it as defining the limits of reality. However, the Christian way of seeing things is not about running away from a real world that we can see, touch and feel, into some kind of unreal ghostly world. Rather, it is about realizing that *this* is the ghostly world that must give way to a fuller and richer renewed creation. What we see around us is the shadow; reality in all its fullness has yet to come.

It's a bit like *The Matrix* (1999). This highly original film develops the idea that we live in a world that feels totally real to us, and which we accept as defining our limits. Yet anyone who is able to step outside it and look at it from this new perspective realizes the truth – that our world is pale, insipid and shadowy in comparison to the greater reality of the world that surrounds it. It is a simulation, a copy, of a greater reality. And once we have seen that greater reality, we can look at our own world of time and space with new eyes and see it for what it really is. It's hard not to observe the parallels with a Christian way of thinking here.

Let's revisit Plato's analogy of the cave once more (p. 23). Remember, that analogy asks us to imagine people imprisoned all their lives in an underground cave, who see and know only a world of shadows. The cave is real enough. It's just that the prisoners don't know that a greater reality lies beyond its walls. They believe that its flickering shadows define both the nature and limits of reality. What they think is *home* is actually a *prison*. Yet this is an insight that you can only gain by stepping outside the cave and seeing what lies beyond it.

So imagine that someone arrives in the shadowlands of the cave from this outside world. He draws a map that allows the cave-dwellers to see that their gloomy cavern is actually part of a greater reality. He offers to lead them from its shadows into the bright and brilliant world beyond. That, in a nutshell, is what the Christian themes of revelation and salvation are all about. Jesus of Nazareth both shows us the way things really are, and makes possible a new way of life.

This is a leading theme of John's Gospel, which speaks of Jesus of Nazareth as the 'true light that enlightens everyone', who came 'into the world' (John 1.9). In Jesus Christ 'the Word became flesh and lived among us' (John 1.14). He is the 'light of the world' (John 8.12; 9.5), who allows us to see our world for what it really is, and points to another world, where we truly belong and where a place has been prepared for us. We will consider these ideas in more detail in the third volume of this series.

Plato's image of the cave helps us grasp three key aspects of Christian faith – acceptance, trust and transformation. We thought we were confined to a dark, smoky cave. We believed that this was the totality of existence. Then a stranger entered and told us otherwise. He illuminated our understanding and we began to see our situation in a very different light. We started to accept that there might be another world – a better world, where we really belong. If the stranger is to be trusted, we are prisoners who have just been offered freedom. For the stranger promises to take us from bondage to liberty, from darkness to light. Is the stranger trustworthy? Do we really want to be free? (Would it be a lot less scary to stay where we are?)

Or to put it in a slightly different way: in the light of the Christian faith, we realize that we are broken, wounded and in need of healing. On its own, that insight could be devastating, but there is good news. One of the reasons why the first Christians used the Greek word *evangelion* ('good news') to speak about their faith was that they believed it offered *hope*. The 'God of hope' reveals the uncomfortable truth about our situation. Yet God can change things. The gospel speaks of both our *illumination* and our *transformation*. We are told that we are ill; yet we are also reassured that there is a cure, which we are invited to accept. We are told that we are in prison, but we are reassured that there is a redeemer who can throw open the gates so that we may go free – and go home. And we are invited to accept and embrace this hope.

The point is clear. We can look at this world in different ways. Those whose creed is 'what you see is what you get' picture a one-way street leading inexorably to death and decay: 'Eat, drink and be merry, for tomorrow we die.' Christians look at the same world, but because we are viewing it in the light of the great themes of the Christian faith, we see it quite differently. It is not that we *invent* meaning, but that we are enabled to *discern* it. We simply see things *as they really are*.

After his conversion to Christianity in 1931, C. S. Lewis wrote an allegorical account of the new way of seeing and thinking that now shaped his life. *The Pilgrim's Regress* (1933) is rightly regarded as one of his most difficult books but it is one that repays the patient reader. In it, Lewis tells the story of a 'pilgrim' – a thinly disguised version of himself – who feels drawn to a mysterious island that he realizes is his heart's desire. After a long journey, during which he is accompanied by a Guide, he finally arrives at this island. It is a transforming moment, but the time comes when he must return home, retracing his steps, and this is when the book gets really interesting.

When the 'pilgrim' walks back through the same landscape after coming to faith – the 'regress' of the book's title – he discovers that its appearance seems to have changed. His Guide explains that he is now 'seeing the land as it really is'. He has been given new eyes. 'Your eyes are altered. You see nothing now but realities.'[3]

Lewis is here trying to put into words the biblical notion that an encounter with the living God transforms our vision. Three striking images are used in the New Testament to help us understand this point: a veil is removed from our eyes; our sight is healed; and scales fall from our eyes. In every case, a barrier to seeing things as they really are is done away with. And once we see things rightly, this will naturally affect the way we live.

The balcony and the road

To explore this point further, let's look at a classic analogy that many have thought helpful, which is found in the writings of John Alexander Mackay (1889–1983). Mackay was a Scottish theologian whose distinguished career led him to become President of Princeton Theological Seminary. When still in his mid-twenties, he spent a year in Madrid learning the Spanish language in preparation for missionary work in Latin America. The famous analogy he developed, which contrasts the views from the 'balcony' and the 'road',[4] occurred to him as he watched Spaniards relaxing after dinner in Madrid and Salamanca (an ancient university town a little over 100 miles north-west of the capital). Let's see what he had in mind.

Imagine a street in a Spanish town, on a warm evening. Some people are walking along, talking about life; others are seated on the balconies of houses, high above the streets, looking down on the bustling scenes below. Their elevated vantage point allows them to overhear the conversations of the people walking along as they go about their business. The people on the balcony are spectators of, not participants in, the stream of life that is passing below them on the street.

Mackay came to see the 'balcony' and the 'road' as two different 'perspectives' or ways of thinking about the Christian faith. The balcony represented 'the perfect spectator, for whom life and the universe are permanent objects of study and contemplation'. Faith gives us a new vantage point, allowing us a fresh way of seeing things. As we've explored, this is unquestionably one of the core themes of the Christian faith.

Yet Mackay believed that the real place of faith was on the 'road', where 'choices are made and decisions are carried out'. Here, faith is about a way of living – about taking decisions about what to do, where to turn and how to live. Those on the balcony are onlookers; those on the road are travellers. The people on the balcony might watch people moving about below, and speculate idly on where these people were going, what they were worried about or where the road led to. But when you are on the road, these are not idle speculative questions. They are real and important. For Mackay, the Christian faith belongs on the road. Faith is not just about making sense of things; it is about obedience, as we try to live out our faith as we travel.

Take the problem of suffering. From the balcony, making sense of suffering is like a logical puzzle. How can a good God allow suffering? On the road, coping with suffering is a very real concern. How can we keep going in the face of suffering? How can we support others in the same situation, while also finding comfort and compassion?

The view from the balcony matters! It offers us a 'big picture' that helps us make sense of the detail we see below. It's as if we have a map of the landscape. But you can't be content with studying a map all the time. There's more to life than thinking. Sooner or later, we need to travel. To explore. To journey. To *live*. The map reassures us that there is indeed a road on which we may travel and a destination that we may finally reach. The map helps us along the way, but our position – most of the time at least – is on the road, as we journey to that destination.

This helps explain why so many people find Christian biographies more helpful and interesting than works of theology. Biographies tell the story of a lived life, of someone who has worked out how to cope with the life of faith, and can pass on a legacy of advice, wisdom and encouragement. 'Here's a problem I encountered. And here's what I found helpful. Maybe it will help you as well.' Theological books can – though many do not – enable their readers to make more sense of things. But that's for the balcony. On the road, we need travelling companions – people who have walked the walk of faith before us, and who can pass on to us the wisdom they picked up along the way.

We can look to the past for examples of such wisdom to help us on our road. There are many who have done this journey and left us notes to encourage and guide us as we follow after them. The great Scottish preacher Horatius

Bonar (1808–89), best known for his hymns 'Fill thou my life, O Lord my God' and 'I heard the voice of Jesus say', is one. Bonar knew a lot about suffering, not as an abstract theological question, but as a living reality. Five of his children died while they were still young. He struggled to make sense of this, and found comfort in focusing his thoughts on the compassion of God, who entered into this suffering world in Christ.

> We are made partakers of Christ's sufferings. What honour is this! We are baptized with His baptism; we drink of His cup, we are made like Him in sorrow as we shall hereafter be made like Him in joy! How soothing and sustaining! If reproach, and shame, and poverty are ours, let us remember that they were His also. If we have to go down to Gethsemane, or up to the cross, let us think that He was there before us.[5]

But we do not need to look only to the past for wisdom and consolation. Mackay's analogy of the balcony and the road reminds us of the importance of other believers around us *now*, offering us comfort and encouragement as we journey along the road together. We share how we cope with loss and bereavement; with disappointment and failure; and with success and joy. That's the way it's meant to be. We'll have more to say about this in the fourth and fifth volumes in this series.

Believing and behaving

So how does a Christian way of seeing things affect how we live? One of the simplest and most important ethical insights is that the way we see something shapes how we act towards it. I remember visiting a school friend many years ago, and being attacked by his pet dog. It was bad-tempered, mangy and very old. He apologized for its behaviour. It had belonged to his beloved grandmother, and she had asked him, just before she died a year earlier, to look after her dog for the rest of its life. To me, it was just a nasty old dog. To him, it was a link with his past, the beloved pet of a beloved relative and very special to him.

I'm sure everyone reading this will recognize the issue. I saw my friend's dog as a problem to be avoided. He saw that same dog as something his grandmother had entrusted to him. He was accountable for it. Our view of that same animal was very different.

Let's go back to Canford School and its block of stone (p. 26). Most people looked at the stone and regarded it as a nuisance, having no value other than for propping up a dartboard. Then someone saw it for what it really was, and realized its true value. Suddenly, a problem became a treasure. From that moment onwards, it was handled with the greatest care!

How we see life affects the way we behave. One of the things that the Roman authorities noticed about the early Christians was their willingness to accept martyrdom for their faith. The Roman authorities regularly imposed the death sentence for taking part in Christian worship or for refusing to worship the emperor. Yet those first Christians would rather die than renounce their faith. Why? *Because of the way they saw life.* Life was something important and immensely worthwhile – but it was transcended by the hope of heaven. Cyprian of Carthage, a bishop who was martyred for his faith in 258 (p. 14), expressed this point well.

We live here as strangers and pilgrims. Let us embrace the day which assigns each of us to our own homeland – which restores each of us to paradise and the kingdom of heaven, snatching us from this place, and setting us free from the restrictions of this world. Which one of us, when in a foreign country, would not hasten to return to our native land?[6]

Cyprian's words paint a big picture that allows life and death to be seen in a new light – with implications for the way in which Christians behave. The Christian mode of thinking about this world invites us to see ourselves as 'citizens of heaven' who are in exile on earth, but with the firm hope of return to our homeland.

This theme of exile plays a major role in Christian spirituality, giving us a framework for making sense of our situation and sustaining faith and hope as we journey. As a way of conceiving the Christian life, it is modelled on the exile of most of the population of Jerusalem to Babylon during the sixth century before Christ. The Babylonian conquerors of Judea were determined to punish the people for their rebelliousness, but those in exile were sustained through the long, harsh years of exile by an equal determination to keep alive both memories of their homeland and the hope of return. The familiar words of Psalm 137.1 capture this sense of longing:

By the rivers of Babylon we sat down and wept,
when we remembered Zion.

The Christian big picture helps us realize that we are exiles on earth – in a cave, to revert to Plato's analogy – cut off from our homeland, and looking forward eagerly to going home, which is where we really belong. The Christian life is thus poised between past and future, sustained by *memory* on the one hand and *expectancy* on the other. We are invited to remember and anticipate. In the past, we recall the great act of redemption by which God delivered us from sin, death and despair through the cross and resurrection of Jesus Christ. And in the future, we eagerly look forward to our entry into the New Jerusalem.

This gives us a framework for living on earth. There are things that need to be done here – such as caring for others and serving God. There are things that are to be enjoyed here – such as the beauty of nature and the company and comfort of family and friends. But these are to be seen as anticipating something still greater and better. C. S. Lewis made the point well: we must be careful 'never to despise, or be unthankful for, these earthly blessings, and on the other, never to mistake them for the something else of which they are only a kind of copy, or echo, or mirage'.[7] The copy is good; but the real thing is still better. And when the time comes to leave echoes and mirages behind, we should do so gladly, knowing that we move from the good to the best.

When I was young, I was forced to learn some poems. I think my schoolteachers considered them to be 'improving', and rather optimistically hoped that they would make me into a better person. One of these was attributed to the Irish poet Frederick Langbridge (1849–1922), and went something like this:

> Two men look out through the same prison bars,
> One sees the mud, the other the stars.

People can be in the same situation yet have a very different outlook. Our creed shapes what we see. Some look down and see only the 'mud' – the rut of a meaningless life, ending in an equally meaningless death. But others look up and see the 'stars' – and as Christians we are reminded to let our hearts soar heavenwards, where Jesus of Nazareth has gone before to prepare a place for us (Colossians 3.1–4).

We could easily give other examples to make the same point. The Christian big picture calls into question the true value of things that this world values highly – such as wealth and personal status. Somehow, their currency seems to have been devalued. Instead, we learn to value serving others and take pleasure in caring for those whom the world regards as insignificant. 'Christianity preaches the infinite worth of that which is seemingly worthless and the infinite worthlessness of that which is seemingly so valued' (Dietrich Bonhoeffer).

Again, some people see the earth as a resource that is there for their convenience. We can do what we like with it. Yet the Christian doctrine of creation reminds us that this earth is not ours. It is God's, and has been entrusted to us, as its stewards. This gives us a quite different framework for our ethical reflections!

Faith in Christ: early Christian imagery

The early Christians have accompanied us through much of this volume. As we continue to consider our own journey through life, there's a good deal to be gained by drawing on some of the representations of Jesus of Nazareth – the 'image of the invisible God' (Colossians 1.15) – that they used to help them reflect on their faith.[8]

Forced underground by the hostility of the Roman Empire, the early Christians dug down into the soft basaltic rock beneath Rome and constructed long tunnels. These became places to meet for prayer and worship and to bury their dead. The Christians covered the walls of these catacombs with powerful images, the best known of which is probably the fish. Why use a fish as a symbol of their faith? Well, apart from being easily drawn, the Greek word for 'fish' is *ichthus*, and i-ch-th-u-s are the initial letters of the Greek words that spell out 'Jesus Christ, son of God, Saviour' – a very handy bullet-point summary of faith.

Other ways of representing Christ can be found in the catacombs. For example, he is sometimes drawn in a highly stylized way with a halo, similar to the Roman pagan 'Sun God'. This image reminded and reassured believers that Jesus is the 'light of the world' (John 8.12) whose coming has displaced and overshadowed the pagan gods.

We shall focus here on another two images that were clearly of considerable importance to early Christians as they considered the journey of faith amid difficult and dangerous circumstances. These images are sometimes found together on Christian sarcophagi (the large stone coffins in which the dead were placed). The first image portrays Christ as a philosopher, holding the trademark philosopher's travelling staff in one hand and a gospel in the other. In classical culture, a philosopher was a teacher of wisdom, whose instruction enabled people to live and die well. With his staff, Christ conquers death; with his gospel, he brings the truth that philosophers had long searched for, but is now fulfilled in his coming, enabling us to see things as they really are.

The second image portrays Christ as the good shepherd (John 10.14) carrying lambs on his shoulders (Luke 15.4–5). The shepherd cares for his sheep because they are his own; he is willing to seek out those that get lost and carry them home when they are exhausted or wounded. It is not difficult to understand the power that this symbol of divine compassion, care and commitment must have had in a Roman cultural environment that was often intensely hostile to those who held such beliefs. That symbol can speak deeply to Christians today, especially when they feel under threat from an intolerant culture.

Both these images help us understand how the early Christians understood their faith: it was about steadfastly and obediently entrusting themselves to Jesus Christ. They placed themselves under his authority. He brought meaning and order to their lives, and was with them at all times, even when they paid the ultimate price for their devotion. It is impossible for us to read about the life and faith of Christians in second- and third-century Rome without feeling challenged. Our devotion can seem but a shadow of that of our distant relatives on the family tree of faith. Those early Christians, though long dead, have much to say to us about the life-changing quality of the gospel.

They, like the first disciples on the shores of Lake Galilee, found in Jesus Christ someone and something so compelling that they responded with everything they had. At their secret meetings on Sundays, they would hear the Gospel accounts of the words and deeds of Jesus read aloud to them, and try to model their lives accordingly. His ways would be their ways. His God would be their God. It is no accident that the New Testament speaks of 'the God and Father of our Lord Jesus Christ' (2 Corinthians 1.3; 1 Peter 1.3).

Yet another symbol that appears frequently in the catacombs, this time to represent the hope of the Christian faith, is an anchor. The New Testament speaks of 'a sure and steadfast anchor of the soul', connecting the believer with the risen Christ (Hebrews 6.19). This clearly struck a chord with those early Christians. Though their earthly lives were full of uncertainties, they were anchored in a place of safety, like a ship that has returned from stormy seas to a sheltered harbour. They knew the secure connection that exists between the everyday world of the believer and another world – one into which Christ has already gone, as the first-fruits of those who will follow him.

Why did this image sear itself into the imaginations of the early Christians? Why did it speak so powerfully to them in times of danger and distress? Perhaps the simplest answer is that it is a symbol of connection. It reassures believers that they are connected with the risen Christ; that there is a firm and unbreakable link between their own world and a deeper reality. This 'hope' is not a vague and faltering aspiration ('I hope the world will become a better place'), but a firm and confident trust that, whatever life may bring, we have found a rock on which to stand. As Augustine of Hippo put it in the early fifth century: 'I live in God. There you should fix your hope, there is the anchor of your heart, so that the tempests of the world will not tear you away.'[9]

Faith, hope and love

As we have seen, Christian faith is about far more than just 'belief' – for example, belief that there is a God. As we come to the end of this introductory volume, it may be helpful to summarize the points we have explored and to develop them a little further.

First, Christian faith is about discerning the big picture that is laid out in the Bible and the creeds, realizing how good it is, how much sense it makes, and gradually finding that we are viewing the world in a completely different way.

Remember the little telescope I mentioned in Chapter 1? It was built from old camera lenses that were lying around our house. When the skies were clear (it rains a lot in Northern Ireland), I could see the moons of the planet Jupiter and track the movements of the planets against the background of the stars. Once I tracked the movement of the planet Mars for a period of weeks. I couldn't make sense of what I saw. Mars drifted eastwards for several nights, then seemed to stop and move westwards. Eventually, it moved eastwards again.[10] I was baffled.

I asked my science teacher to explain this and he drew diagrams to show me the relative motions of the earth and Mars. After about five minutes, I got it. I could see what was happening. The penny dropped. *But someone had to tell me.* My teacher gave me a framework for understanding what I had seen, and it made perfect sense. Why didn't I think of that myself, I wondered.

But that's what revelation is all about. It's about being given a big picture that we couldn't conceive ourselves. And once we are given it, we discover just how much sense it makes. Theologians talk about faith being both 'beyond reason' and 'reasonable'. What they mean by that is that it's not something that we could work out completely for ourselves. We need to be *told* and *shown* the way things really are. Yet once we have been given this way of seeing things, we discover just how much sense it makes.

Part of the process of growing in faith is coming to appreciate the spiritual vitality of this deeper understanding of things. In one sense, this aspect of faith is primarily about intellectual acceptance. Although we can't prove that this new way of seeing things is right, it makes so much sense that we are prepared to commit ourselves to living on its basis, knowing that millions before us have found it reliable and resilient. Reciting the creeds is about holding hands with those who've walked before us along the road of faith and talked through its great themes.

This naturally leads into the second element of faith: trusting this God and this way of thinking, and exploring its implications. It is about realizing that a 'surface reading' of things is simply inadequate. There is a big picture to be discovered that goes far beyond the limited and impoverished view of things that results from skimming the surface of reality. The creed of many around us may be 'what you see is what you get'. Yet we are called to go 'further up and further in', and help others raise their horizons and open their eyes to a deeper and richer understanding of reality.

Third, faith is about the way we live. It is about entering into and acting in accordance with this bigger picture, aligning ourselves with its vision of reality. Christian morality does not need to borrow ideas to help it work out what is right and wrong; these are all contained within its big picture. Our task is to explore the moral landscape of our faith and allow it to illuminate and inform our actions.

Instead of passively accepting the ways of thinking that we find around us, we develop a way of seeing reality that is based on the Christian faith itself. 'Do not be conformed to this world, but be transformed by the renewing of your minds' (Romans 12.2). Faith is about transforming our hopes, values and expectations in the light of the new way of seeing things that the Christian faith makes possible. Who we are shapes what we see. Christianity changes who we are, so that we see things with new eyes and in new ways.

Fourth, Christian faith is not limited to accepting things the way they are. It proclaims, joyfully and confidently, that they can be changed. Yes, we are sinners, but we can become forgiven and transformed sinners. Yes, we are mortal, but we are offered the right to enter the New Jerusalem and dwell as honoured citizens within its courts. Faith and hope are closely linked in the Christian proclamation, for both are grounded in the trustworthiness and graciousness of God. 'May the God of hope fill you with all joy and peace in believing, so that you may abound in hope by the power of the Holy Spirit' (Romans 15.13).

And fifth, Christian faith leads to changed conduct. It affects the way we live. When writing to the Christian community in Rome, Paul expresses his delight that their faith was known throughout the inhabited world of his day (Romans 1.8). In that same letter, he rejoices that their *obedience* was also celebrated (Romans 16.19). Paul brings these ideas together in speaking of the 'obedience of faith' (Romans 1.5; 16.26) – a Greek phrase that almost certainly means something like 'the obedience which springs from faith' or 'the obedience which is based on faith'.

Paradoxically, belief in heaven does not lead Christians to disengage from the world, as some poorly informed critics suggest. A vision of the New Jerusalem makes us yearn to bring about at least some of its values and attributes in our own age, trying to shape the present in the light of God's coming kingdom. If heaven is to be a place in which there is no longer any pain (Revelation 21.4), why not try to do something about the suffering we see around us now? It is no accident that so many Christians find themselves drawn to medical and humanitarian work, seeing this as part of the big picture of the Christian faith.

Moving on

We have used the image of a beautiful and mysterious landscape several times in this introductory volume. In the next four books we will be exploring its forests and rivers, its valleys and mountains. We have already seen how the Christian faith is like a lens, bringing this landscape into sharper focus. It is like a map that helps us make sense of the terrain over which we are travelling. It is like a light that illuminates our path ahead of us and the shadowlands around us.

We paused and lingered, tantalizingly, over the opening words of the creed: 'I believe'. We are now ready to move on and explore more fully what comes next – the Christian vision of God.

Appendix

The Apostles' Creed and the Nicene Creed

The Apostles' Creed

I believe in God, the Father almighty,
creator of heaven and earth.

I believe in Jesus Christ, God's only Son, our Lord,
who was conceived by the Holy Spirit,
born of the Virgin Mary,
suffered under Pontius Pilate,
was crucified, died, and was buried;
he descended to the dead.
On the third day he rose again;
he ascended into heaven,
he is seated at the right hand of the Father,
and he will come to judge the living and the dead.

I believe in the Holy Spirit,
the holy catholic Church,
the communion of saints,
the forgiveness of sins,
the resurrection of the body,
and the life everlasting.
Amen.[1]

The Nicene Creed

We believe in one God,
the Father, the Almighty,
maker of heaven and earth,
of all that is,
seen and unseen.

We believe in one Lord, Jesus Christ,
the only Son of God,
eternally begotten of the Father,
God from God, Light from Light,
true God from true God,
begotten, not made,
of one Being with the Father;
through him all things were made.
For us and for our salvation he came down from heaven,
was incarnate of the Holy Spirit and the Virgin Mary
and became truly human.
For our sake he was crucified under Pontius Pilate;
he suffered death and was buried.
On the third day he rose again
in accordance with the Scriptures;
he ascended into heaven
and is seated at the right hand of the Father.
He will come again in glory to judge the living and the
    dead,
and his kingdom will have no end.

We believe in the Holy Spirit, the Lord, the giver of life,
who proceeds from the Father and the Son,
who with the Father and the Son is worshipped and
    glorified,
who has spoken through the prophets.

We believe in one holy catholic and apostolic Church.
We acknowledge one baptism for the forgiveness of sins.
We look for the resurrection of the dead,
and the life of the world to come.
Amen.[2]

Notes

1 The journey: clues to the meaning of the universe

1 Jean-Paul Sartre, *Nausea*. New York: New Directions Publishing, 1964, 180.
2 Sartre, *Nausea*, 157.
3 Richard Dawkins, *River Out of Eden: A Darwinian View of Life*. London: Phoenix, 1995, 133.
4 Christopher Hitchens, *God is Not Great*. New York: Twelve, 2007, 5.
5 Richard Dawkins, *A Devil's Chaplain*. London: Weidenfeld & Nicolson, 2003, 34.
6 Max Weber, 'Wissenschaft als Beruf', in *Gesammelte Aufsätze zur Wissenschaftslehre*. Tübingen: J. C. B. Mohr, 1922, 524–55.
7 C. S. Lewis, *Surprised by Joy*. London: HarperCollins, 2002, 197.
8 See Alister E. McGrath, *C. S. Lewis: A Life*. London: Hodder & Stoughton, 2013.
9 C. S. Lewis, *Collected Letters Volume One: Family Letters 1905–31*, ed. Walter Hooper. London: HarperCollins, 2009.
10 Lewis, *Surprised by Joy*, 221–2.
11 Austin Farrer, 'The Christian Apologist', in *Light on C. S. Lewis*, ed. Jocelyn Gibb. London: Geoffrey Bles, 1965, 26.
12 Michael Polanyi, *The Tacit Dimension*. Garden City, NY: Doubleday, 1967, 24.
13 David Brewster, *Life of Sir Isaac Newton*, new edn, revised W. T. Lynn, London: Tegg, 1875, 303.
14 Augustine of Hippo, *Confessions*, I.1.1.

15 Fyodor Dostoyevsky, *The Dream of a Ridiculous Man*. New York: Modern Library, 1992, 335.

16 Letter to Colette O'Niel, 23 October 1916, *The Selected Letters of Bertrand Russell: The Public Years 1914–1970*. London: Routledge, 2001, 85.

17 Katharine Tait, *My Father Bertrand Russell*. New York: Harcourt Brace Jovanovich, 1975, 189.

18 C. S. Lewis, *Mere Christianity*. London: HarperCollins, 2002, 135.

19 Virginia Woolf, 'A Sketch of the Past', in *Moments of Being*, ed. Jeanne Schulkind, 2nd edn. New York: Harcourt Brace & Co., 1985, 72.

20 Frederick Buechner, *Wishful Thinking*. New York: HarperCollins, 1993, 120.

21 Lewis, *Mere Christianity*, 136–7.

22 Richard Rorty, *Consequences of Pragmatism*. Minneapolis: University of Minneapolis Press, 1982, xlii.

23 Lewis, *Mere Christianity*, 21.

24 Benito Mussolini, *Diuturna, 1914–1922: Scritti polemici*. Milan: Casa Editrice Imperia, 1924, 376–8. I have translated the Italian term *mentalità* as 'ideology'; it can also be translated as 'mentality' or 'intellectual outlook'.

25 Iris Murdoch, 'Vision and Choice in Morality', *Proceedings of the Aristotelian Society*, Supplementary Volume 30 (1956): 32–58.

26 Humphrey Carpenter, *W. H. Auden: A Biography*. Boston, MA: Houghton Mifflin Co., 1981, 282–3.

27 G. K. Chesterton, *The Everlasting Man*. San Francisco: Ignatius Press, 1993, 105.

28 Plato, *Republic*, 514a–520a.

2 The map, the lens and the light: making sense of things

1 John M. Russell, *From Nineveh to New York: The Strange Story of the Assyrian Reliefs in the Metropolitan Museum and the Hidden*

Masterpiece at Canford School. New Haven, CT: Yale University Press, 1997, 173–89.

2 William James, *The Will to Believe.* New York: Dover Publications, 1956, 51.

3 C. S. Lewis, *An Experiment in Criticism.* Cambridge: Cambridge University Press, 1992, 140–1.

4 Letter to Edward Sackville-West, cited in Michael de-la-Noy, *Eddy: The Life of Edward Sackville-West.* London: Bodley Head, 1988, 237.

5 *Macbeth*, V, 5.

6 'The Elixir', in F. E. Hutchinson, *The Works of George Herbert.* Oxford: Oxford University Press, 1941, 184.

7 Iris Murdoch, *The Sovereignty of Good.* London: Routledge, 2001, 82.

8 C. S. Lewis, 'Is Theology Poetry?', in *C. S. Lewis: Essay Collection.* London: Collins, 2000, 21.

9 G. K. Chesterton, 'The Return of the Angels', *Daily News*, 14 March, 1903.

10 Simone Weil, *First and Last Notebooks.* London: Oxford University Press, 1970, 147.

3 Words and stories: discovering the deeper significance of faith

1 Ludwig Wittgenstein, *Remarks on the Philosophy of Psychology.* Oxford: Blackwell, 1980, vol. 2, 687.

2 G. K. Chesterton, *Orthodoxy.* New York: Doubleday, 1956, 78.

3 Alister E. McGrath, *C. S. Lewis: A Life.* London: Hodder & Stoughton, 2013, 335–6.

4 Dorothy L. Sayers, *Creed or Chaos?* London: Methuen, 1947, 24.

5 G. K. Chesterton, *Orthodoxy.* New York: Doubleday, 1956, 11.

6 Dorothy L. Sayers, 'Creative Mind', in *Unpopular Opinions.* New York: Harcourt Brace & Co., 1947, 49.

7 Frederick Buechner, *Wishful Thinking*. New York: HarperCollins, 1993, 76.

4 The creeds: a public vision of faith

1 C. S. Lewis, *Surprised by Joy*. London: HarperCollins, 2002, 265.

2 Lewis, *Surprised by Joy*, 264.

3 Tertullian, *On the Prescription of Heretics*, 13. Tertullian hints at Hebrews 1.1–2 in this passage: 'Long ago God spoke to our ancestors in many and various ways by the prophets, but in these last days he has spoken to us by a Son.'

4 Cyril of Jerusalem, *Catechesis* V, 12.

5 *The Martyrdom of Justin*, 1.

6 John of Salisbury, *Metalogicon*, iii, 4.

7 C. S. Lewis, *An Experiment in Criticism*. Cambridge: Cambridge University Press, 1992, 137.

8 C. S. Lewis, 'On the Reading of Old Books', in *C. S. Lewis: Essay Collection*. London: HarperCollins, 2001, 440.

9 Dorothy L. Sayers, *Creed or Chaos?* London: Methuen, 1947, 33.

5 'I believe': stepping into the 'big picture'

1 Martin Luther, *Great Catechism* (1529), III.1.

2 Dietrich Bonhoeffer, *Life Together: A Discussion of Christian Fellowship*. New York: Harper & Row, 1954, 28.

3 C. S. Lewis, *The Pilgrim's Regress*, London: Geoffrey Bles, 1950, 176–7.

4 John A. Mackay, *A Preface to Christian Theology*. London: Nisbet, 1942, 27–53.

5 Horatius Bonar, *The Night of Weeping*. New York: Carter, 1864, 164–5.

6 Cyprian of Carthage, *On Mortality*, 7, 25.

7 C. S. Lewis, *Mere Christianity*. London: HarperCollins, 2002, 137.

8 Jon A. B. Jongeneel, *Jesus Christ in World History*. New York: Peter Lang, 2009, 94.

9 Augustine of Hippo, *Sermon* 177, 8.

10 Technically, this is known as the 'retrograde motion' of the planets, which arises when the earth overtakes the outer planets in the course of its annual orbit of the sun.

Appendix: The Apostles' Creed and the Nicene Creed

1 *Common Worship: Services and Prayers for the Church of England,* London: Church House Publishing, 2000, 35.

2 Adapted by the author from *Common Worship*, 173.

A short booklist

The following are useful studies of the creeds and some of their themes:

Hans Urs von Balthasar, *Credo: Meditations on the Apostles' Creed*. San Francisco: Ignatius Press, 2000.

Roger van Harn, ed., *Exploring and Proclaiming the Apostles' Creed*. Grand Rapids, MI: Eerdmans, 2004.

Luke Timothy Johnson, *The Creed: What Christians Believe and Why It Matters*. New York: Doubleday, 2003.

J. N. D. Kelly, *Early Christian Creeds*, 3rd edn. New York: Continuum, 2006.

C. S. Lewis, *Mere Christianity*. London: Collins, 2002.

Henri de Lubac, *The Christian Faith: An Essay on the Structure of the Apostles' Creed*. San Francisco: Ignatius Press, 1986.

Alister E. McGrath, *Heresy: A History of Defending the Truth*. London: SPCK, 2009.

Oliver C. Quick, *Doctrines of the Creed: Their Basis in Scripture and Their Meaning Today*. London: Nisbet, 1938.

Dorothy L. Sayers, *Creed or Chaos?* London: Methuen, 1947.

J. S. Whale, *Christian Doctrine*. Cambridge: Cambridge University Press, 1941.

Rowan Williams, *Tokens of Trust: An Introduction to Christian Belief*. Norwich: Canterbury Press, 2007.

Tom Wright, *Simply Christian*. London: SPCK, 2006.

Frances Young, *The Making of the Creeds*. London: SCM Press, 2002.

If you would like to begin studying Christian theology as a way of taking the themes of this series further, you might like to try these introductions, both of which can be used without the need for a teacher:

Alister E. McGrath, *Christian Theology: An Introduction*, 5th edn. Oxford and Malden, MA: Wiley-Blackwell, 2010.

Alister E. McGrath, *The Christian Theology Reader*, 4th edn. Oxford and Malden, MA: Wiley-Blackwell, 2011.